What Readers Are Saying About De

Paul does an excellent job of explaining the technical, intellectual, and psychological aspects of all phases of debugging: preventing bugs in the first place, diagnosing and fixing bugs, and making sure that the same bugs don't happen again. Applying any or all of the ideas from this book will improve the overall quality of your software projects.

Sure, the technical issues are well covered but how Paul also explains the psychological angles is what makes this book exceptional.

► **Frederic Daoud**
Author, *Stripes...and Java Web Development Is Fun Again*

I wholeheartedly recommend this book to software engineers generally but more specifically to team leads who need to know how to set up their teams for best practice.

► **Allan McLeod**
Founder and CTO, Isaacc Software

Debug It! does a great job of setting the scene for debugging and getting you into the right mind-set while also talking about the complications that can arise once the bug is found and squashed. It's worth a look for the anecdotes alone, to see the lengths that people go to when trying to understand truly bizarre defects.

► **Jon Dickinson**
Author, *Grails 1.1 Web Application Development*

Debugging has been a folk art for so long that it's great to have someone put all the tried-and-true techniques together. *Debug It!* is the perfect book to pull out when you're disillusioned with the brain-breaking process of creating good software. With this tool chest of assertions, logging, refactoring, and other good stuff, you'll feel like you're Sherlock Holmes and solving the case is inevitable.

► **Craig Riecke**
Author, *Mastering Dojo: JavaScript and Ajax Tools for Great Web Experiences*

This book is like a companion volume to *The Pragmatic Programmer*, applying the same focus on craftsmanship to the debugging process.

► **Ian Dees**
Author, *Scripted GUI Testing with Ruby*

Paul Butcher has brought long overdue attention to the methods of debugging, a fundamental activity for every software developer yet one that remains an exercise of intuition and guesswork for most in the profession. Paul's gentle writing style belies the discipline in his technique. Before you know it, you'll be an engineer instead of a hacker.

► **Bill Karwin**
Software Engineer, Karwin Software Solutions, LLC

Debug It!

Find, Repair, and Prevent Bugs in Your Code

Find, Repair, and Preven

Paul Butcher

The Pragmatic Bookshelf
Raleigh, North Carolina   Dallas, Texas

Many of the designations used by manufacturers and sellers to distinguish their products are claimed as trademarks. Where those designations appear in this book, and The Pragmatic Programmers, LLC was aware of a trademark claim, the designations have been printed in initial capital letters or in all capitals. The Pragmatic Starter Kit, The Pragmatic Programmer, Pragmatic Programming, Pragmatic Bookshelf and the linking *g* device are trademarks of The Pragmatic Programmers, LLC.

Every precaution was taken in the preparation of this book. However, the publisher assumes no responsibility for errors or omissions, or for damages that may result from the use of information (including program listings) contained herein.

Our Pragmatic courses, workshops, and other products can help you and your team create better software and have more fun. For more information, as well as the latest Pragmatic titles, please visit us at

http://www.pragprog.com

ISBN-10: 1-934356-28-X
ISBN-13: 978-1-934356-28-9
Printed on acid-free paper.
P1.0 printing, November 2009
Version: 2009-10-19

Contents

Preface

I've always been mystified why so few books are available on debugging. You can buy any number on every other aspect of software engineering such as design, code construction, requirements capture, methodologies...the list is endless. And yet, for some reason, debugging has been almost (not quite but very nearly) ignored by authors and publishers. I hope that this book can help remedy the situation.

If you write code, it's a certainty that at some point (possibly very soon afterward) you're going to have to debug it. Debugging is, more than anything else, an intellectual process—it doesn't take place within a debugger or your code but inside your mind. Reaching an understanding of the root cause of the problem is the cornerstone upon which everything else depends.

Over the years, I've been fortunate to work with a number of incredibly talented teams on a wide range of software. I've worked at all levels of abstraction from microcode on bit-slice processors through device drivers, embedded code, mainstream desktop software, and web applications. I hope that I can pass along some of the lessons I've learned from my colleagues along the way.

About This Book

This book is divided into three parts, each of which considers a particular aspect of debugging:

"The Heart of the Problem":
>   This part introduces the empirical approach, which leverages our software's unique ability to show us what's going on, and the core debugging method (reproduce, diagnose, fix, reflect) that relies upon it.

"The Bigger Picture":

> How do we find out that there's a problem that needs fixing in the first place? And how does debugging integrate into the wider software development process?

"Debug-Fu":

> In the third and final part, we'll turn our attention to a number of advanced topics:

- Although the approaches discussed earlier in the book apply to all bugs, certain types of bugs benefit from special treatment.

- Debugging starts long before the irate telephone call from the user affected by it. What tools and processes can we put in place ahead of time to help when the phone rings?

- Finally, we'll consider a number of common pitfalls to avoid.

Acknowledgments

It's not until I embarked upon the task of writing a book of my own that I realized the true importance of the acknowledgments section. My name might be on the front cover, but it wouldn't have come to fruition without the help of many and the forbearance of many more.

Thanks to everyone who joined the book's email discussion list and provided inspiration, criticism, and encouragement—Andrew Eacott, Daniel Winterstein, Freeland Abbott, Gary Swanson, Jorge Hernandez, Manuel Castro, Mike Smith, Paul McKibbin and Sam Halliday. Particular thanks to Dave Strauss, Dominic Binks, Frederick Cheung, Marcus Gröber, Sean Ellis, Vandy Massey, Matthew Jacobs, Bill Karwin, and Jeremy Sydik who have kindly allowed me to share their anecdotes and insights with you. Thanks also to Allan McLeod, Ben Coppin, Miguel Oliveira, Neil Eccles, Nick Heudecker, Ron Green, Craig Riecke, Fred Daoud, Ian Dees, Evan Dickinson, Lyle Johnson, Bill Karwin, and Jeremy Sydik for taking the time to participate in technical review.

To my editor, Jackie Carter, thank you for being so patient with a first-time author learning the ropes, and thanks to Dave and Andy for taking the chance.

Apologies to my colleagues at Texperts who have had to endure me talking about nothing but the book for too long (don't worry—I'll get a new race car soon, and then you'll have to endure me talking about that instead). And to my family, sorry for the long evenings and weekends during which I've been incommunicado, and thanks for the support.

Finally, thank you to everyone I've had the privilege of working with over the years. The best aspect of a career in software development is the caliber of the people, and I've been particularly lucky to work with a truly great selection.

Paul Butcher
August 2009
paul@paulbutcher.com

Part I

The Heart of the Problem

Chapter 1

A Method in the Madness

So, your software doesn't work. Now what?

Some developers seem to have a knack of unerringly zeroing in on the root cause of a bug, whereas others thrash around apparently aimlessly and without concrete results. What separates the first group from the second?

In this chapter, we will examine a debugging method that has been repeatedly proven in the trenches of professional software development. It's not a silver bullet—you're still going to have to rely on your intellect, intuition, detective skills, and, yes, even a little luck. But it will allow you to target your efforts most effectively, avoid chasing phantoms, and get to the heart of the problem as quickly as possible.

Specifically, we'll cover the following:

- The difference between debugging and "making the bug go away"

- The empirical approach—using the software itself to show you what's going on

- The core debugging process (reproduce, diagnose, fix, reflect)

- First things first—things to think about before diving in

1.1 Debugging Is More Than "Making the Bug Go Away"

Ask an inexperienced programmer to define debugging, and they might answer that it is "finding a fix." In fact, that is only one of several goals, and not even the most important of them.

Effective debugging requires that we take these steps:

1. Work out *why* the software is behaving unexpectedly.

2. Fix the problem.

3. Avoid breaking anything else.

4. Maintain or improve the overall quality (readability, architecture, test coverage, performance, and so on) of the code.

5. Ensure that the same problem does not occur elsewhere and cannot occur again.

Of these, by far the most important is the first—identifying the root cause of the problem is the cornerstone upon which everything else depends.

Understanding Is Everything

Inexperienced developers (and sometimes, unfortunately, those of us who should know better) often skip diagnosis altogether. Instead, they immediately implement what they think *might* be a fix. If they're lucky, it won't work, and all they will have done is waste their time. The real danger comes if it works, or seems to work, because now they've made a change to the source that they don't really understand. It might fix the bug, but there is a real chance that in reality it is only masking the true underlying cause. Worse, there is a good chance that this kind of change will introduce *regressions*—breaking something that used to work correctly beforehand.

Wasted Time and Effort

Some years ago, I found myself working in a team containing a number of very experienced and talented developers. Most of their experience was with UNIX, but when I joined the team, they were in the late stages of porting the software to Windows.

One of the bugs found during the port was a performance issue when running many threads simultaneously. Some threads were being starved, while others were running just fine.

Given that everything worked just fine under UNIX, the problem was clearly broken threading in Windows, so the decision was made to implement a custom thread scheduling system and avoid using that provided by the operating system. This would be a lot of work, obviously, but quite within the capabilities of a team of this caliber.

I joined the team when they were some way into the implementation, and sure enough, threads were no longer suffering from starvation. But thread scheduling is subtle, and they were still working through a number of issues that had been caused by the change (not least of which was that the changes had slowed the whole system down somewhat).

I was intrigued by this bug, because I'd previously experienced no problems with Windows' threading. A little investigation demonstrated that the performance issue was caused by the fact that Windows implements a *dynamic thread priority boost*. The bug could be fixed by disabling this with a single line of code (a call to SetThreadPriorityBoost()).

The moral? The team had decided that Windows' threads were broken without really investigating the behavior they were seeing. In part, this might have been a cultural issue—Windows doesn't have a good reputation among UNIX hackers. Nevertheless, if they had taken the time to identify the root cause, they would have saved themselves a great deal of work and avoided introducing complications that made the system both less efficient and more error-prone.

Without first understanding the true root cause of the bug, we are outside the realms of software engineering and delving instead into *voodoo programming*[1] or *programming by coincidence*.[2]

1.2 The Empirical Approach

There are many different approaches you can adopt to gain the understanding you seek. And as long as the approach you choose gets you closer to your goal, it has served its purpose.

Having said that, it turns out that in most instances one particular approach, the *empirical* approach, tends to be by far the most productive.

Empiricism relies upon observation or experience, rather than theory or pure logic. In the context of debugging, this means directly observing the behavior of the software. Yes,

> Construct experiments, and observe the results.

you *could* read the entire source code and use pure reason to work out what's going on (and on occasion you may have no other choice),

---

1. "The use by guess or cookbook of an obscure or hairy system, feature, or algorithm that one does not truly understand. The implication is that the technique may not work, and if it doesn't, one will never know why." Taken from *The Jargon File* [ray].
2. See *The Pragmatic Programmer* [HT00].

> ## On the Nature of Software
>
> Software is remarkable stuff. Sometimes, perhaps because we work with it all the time, we forget just how remarkable it is.
>
> Very little else in human experience is as malleable, allowing us free rein to exercise our ingenuity and inventiveness almost without limits. Also, with a very few exceptions that we'll cover later, software is deterministic—the next state is completely determined by the current state, and (crucially) we have complete access to all of that state whenever we want it.
>
> Compared to traditional engineering, we are spoiled. What do you think a Formula One engineer would give to be able to instantaneously stop an engine when it's rotating at 19,000 revolutions per minute and examine every aspect of it in minute detail? To see the precise state of each component while under pressure and stress, for example, or to dynamically record the shape and position of the flame front within the combustion chambers during ignition?
>
> It is exactly this kind of trick that we are able to perform with our software, which is why the empirical approach is particularly powerful when debugging.

but doing so is usually inefficient and dangerous. You can track the problem down much more effectively by carefully constructing experiments and *observing* how the software behaves. Not only is this faster, but these observations force you to reexamine flawed assumptions in your mental model about how the software behaves. The software itself is the most powerful tool in your toolbox—allow it to *show* you what's going on.

The method described in the next section leverages this approach to provide a structured means of zeroing in on your quarry.

1.3 The Core Debugging Process

The core of the debugging process consists of four steps:

Reproduce:
> Find a way to reliably and conveniently reproduce the problem on demand.

Diagnose:

> Construct hypotheses, and test them by performing experiments until you are confident that you have identified the underlying cause of the bug.

Fix:

> Design and implement changes that fix the problem, avoid introducing regressions, and maintain or improve the overall quality of the software.

Reflect:

> Learn the lessons of the bug. Where did things go wrong? Are there any other examples of the same problem that will also need fixing? What can you do to ensure that the same problem doesn't happen again?

As shown in Figure 1.1, on the following page, broadly speaking, these steps take place one after the other, but this is no strict "waterfall" method. Although you certainly don't want to start upon diagnosis until you have a reproduction or design a fix before you understand the problem, this is an iterative process. Lessons learned during diagnosis might suggest ways to improve your reproduction, or those learned when implementing a fix might cause you to reconsider your diagnosis.

> Debugging is an iterative process.

We'll go into each of these steps in much more detail in the following chapters. Before then, however, there are a few preliminaries to get out of the way.

1.4 First Things First

As tempting as it might be to dive right in, it's worth taking a little time before doing so to make sure that we first have all our ducks in a row.

Do You Know What You're Looking For?

Before you start trying to reproduce the problem or hypothesizing about its cause, you need to know exactly what is happening. And just as important, you need to know what *should* happen instead. If you're working from a formal bug report, it should already contain all the information you need. (We'll talk about bug

> What is happening, and what should?

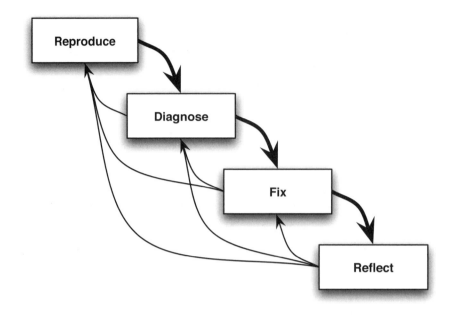

Figure 1.1: Core debugging method

reports in more detail in Chapter 6, *Discovering That You Have a Problem*, on page 89.) Take the time to read it carefully to make sure you understand it.

If you don't have a formal bug report (perhaps you're working on a bug that you've stumbled upon yourself or was reported to you during a watercooler conversation), then it's even more important to pause and make sure that you really can see the full picture before forging ahead.

Remember that bug reports are no less fallible than any other document. Just because the bug report says that *this* should happen instead of *that*, does that really agree with the software's specification? If it's not immediately obvious what the behavior should be, don't make any changes until you've gotten to the bottom of it—changing correct behavior to incorrect, just because the bug report says so, is not going to be helpful.

Battling Bug Reports

I once found myself working on a very simple bug—a report was being generated without taking daylight saving time (DST) into account and was therefore incorrect when the clocks changed. I implemented a nice quick fix, and I moved on to the next problem.

A little later, however, another bug was reported saying that our accountant can't make the books balance. The numbers generated by the report didn't agree with the invoices we were receiving from our suppliers.

Sure enough, it turned out that these invoices didn't take DST into account, which explains the discrepancy. A little historical digging showed that we had already discovered this a year ago, at which point we'd addressed the problem by deliberately ignoring DST.[3]

Clearly, the problem here wasn't that the software wasn't doing what we wanted it to do but that we didn't *know* what we wanted the software to do. Because the report was used in different contexts, in some cases DST should be taken into account, and in others it shouldn't. The correct solution was to add an option to the report to allow the user to choose.

One Problem at a Time

It's sometimes tempting, when faced with several problems, to work on them in parallel. This is especially true if the bugs are all in the same general area. Don't give in to this temptation.

Debugging is difficult enough without "muddying the waters" unnecessarily. However careful you are, there's a good chance that the experiments you perform to try to track down one bug will interfere in some way with the other. This makes it hard to come to a clear understanding of what's happening. In addition (as we will see in Section 4.5, *Checking In*, on page 73), when you eventually come to check in your fix, you want to stick to one check-in per logical change. This is very difficult to achieve if you work on several bugs simultaneously.

Occasionally, you'll find that what you thought was one bug turns out to have more than one root cause. Normally, the point at which this becomes obvious is when you find yourself in the twilight zone—weird things happening that seem to have no obvious explanation. See Section 3.4, *Multiple Causes*, on page 55 for further discussion.

---

3. Incidentally, the developer who originally changed the behavior could have saved us quite a bit of trouble by simply adding a comment in the code explaining why DST was ignored in this instance, making it clear that the behavior was intentional.

Check Simple Things First

Most bugs are caused by simple oversights. Yes, occasionally you will be faced by something very subtle, but don't overlook the simple things.

For some reason, we developers seem to suffer from a feeling that we have to do everything ourselves. This is most obvious in the "Not Invented Here" syndrome in which we end up implementing something ourselves when a perfectly good solution already exists elsewhere. The debugging equivalent of this mistake is assuming that you have to personally debug every problem you encounter.

Asking other team members whether they've seen something similar before is very low cost and yet has the potential to short-circuit a huge amount of wasted effort. This is especially true if you're working in an area you're unfamiliar with.

Subversion Confusion
by Sean Ellis

This week, one of my newer guys was having a particular problem with svn export. Nasty one, this—same version of SVN on the server and his workstation, different behavior, lots of quiet hair pulling.

So, eventually he cracked. He asked me whether there were any problems with this particular command and gave me a cut-and-pasted command line to SVN.

"Yes," I say. There's a defect in the Apache libraries that handles ../../.. in a path wrongly. Two seconds later we confirm that this is indeed the problem, and in a couple of minutes we confirmed that the server has a different version of the Apache runtime DLL.

Of course, much hair pulling had also ensued several months previously while discovering this bug the first time.

So, communication is always important—not just in the odd, subtle, geeky, hard-to-describe ways but in the good old "standing up and asking whether anyone has seen this before" way.

In the next chapter, we'll look at the first step in the process, reproduction, in detail.

1.5 Put It in Action

- Make sure to do the following:

    - Work out *why* the software is behaving unexpectedly.

    - Fix the problem.

    - Avoid breaking anything else.

    - Maintain or improve overall quality.

    - Ensure that the same problem does not occur elsewhere and cannot occur again.

- Leverage your software's ability to *show* you what's happening.

- Work on only one problem at a time.

- Make sure that you know exactly what you're looking for:

    - What is happening?

    - What *should* be happening?

- Check simple things first.

Chapter 2

Reproduce

As we saw in the previous chapter, the empirical approach to debugging leverages your software's unique ability to *show* you what's going on. The key that unlocks this potential is finding a way to reproduce the problem.

In this chapter, we'll cover the following:

- Why finding a reproduction is so important

- How to exert the necessary control over your software to find one

- What makes a good reproduction and how you can close in on this ideal through iterative refinement

2.1 Reproduce First, Ask Questions Later

Why is reproducing the problem so important? Because if you can't, then it's almost impossible to make progress. Specifically:

- The empirical process relies upon our ability to watch the software executing in the presence of the bug. If we can't get the software to misbehave in the first place, then this, the most powerful weapon in our armory, is lost.

- Even if you do somehow manage to come up with a theory about why the software might be misbehaving, how are you going to prove it if you can't reproduce the problem?

- If you think that you've implemented a fix, how are you going to demonstrate that it really does fix the problem?

Not only is it critical to reproduce the problem, but it's critical that this is the *first* thing you do. If you start modifying the source code before you've managed to reproduce the problem, the changes you've made might mask it or introduce some other problem.[1]

So, how exactly do you go about this crucial stage of debugging?

Start with the Obvious

The first thing to try is simply following the steps described (or implied) by the bug report.

This holds true even for a one-line bug report. I've seen developers reject (as "needs more info") a bug report like "Crash on canceling the change password dialog box," without even *trying* to reproduce it. We've all been frustrated by bug reports that don't include vital information, but some bugs simply don't depend upon which operating system you're running, the software's current configuration, what else you were doing at the time, or any of the other boilerplate information your bug report template includes. Try opening the change password dialog box and then hitting Cancel—chances are that the software will crash and you can start your diagnosis without bothering the user for further information. And even if it doesn't, it's not as if you've wasted much time.

If this simplistic approach doesn't bear fruit, then the nature of the bug will provide you with good clues about what to try next.

Targeting Your Effort

Successful reproduction is all about control. If you control all the relevant variables, you *will* reproduce your problem. The trick, of course, is identifying which variables are relevant to the bug at hand, discovering what you need to set them to, and finding a way to do so.

As a developer, your situation is different from your users'. You're working with the very latest source code, whereas they're likely to be running something compiled several weeks, months, or even years ago. Your configuration will be different, as will your network environment, the peripherals you're using, and so on. One or more of these differences are what is stopping the bug from reproducing—your first task, therefore, is to identify and eliminate those differences.

---

1. This is analogous to the rule in test-first development that you shouldn't write any new code until you have a failing test. In this case, your "failing test" is the reproduced bug.

A huge number of things *could* potentially affect the behavior of your software. In most cases, few of them will actually be relevant. How do you know which to concentrate on first?

The things you need to control break down into three areas:[2]

The software itself:
> If the bug is in an area that has changed recently, then ensuring that you're running the same version of the software as it was reported against is a good first step.

The environment it's running within:
> If interaction with an external system (some particular piece of hardware or a remote server perhaps) is involved, then you probably want to ensure that you're using the same.

The inputs you provide to it:
> If the bug is related to an area that behaves very differently depending upon how the software is configured, then start by replicating the user's configuration.

In the following sections, we'll look at each of these areas in more detail.

2.2 Controlling the Software

If you can't immediately reproduce the bug with the latest source code, instead of whatever version the user is running, then it's possible that this is because it has already been fixed. You can't assume that, however—it's just as possible that the bug is still there but in a subtly different form. You can be certain only after you've completed your diagnosis, which starts by finding a reproduction.

Simply compiling from the same source doesn't guarantee that you will be running the same object code. You also need to ensure that you use the same compiler, configured in the same way, and the same runtime, libraries, and any third-party code that is integrated with your software.

Of course, using the same tools gets you nowhere if you don't use them in exactly the right sequence and with the same configuration as the software was originally built with. The best way to ensure that you do

---

2. The boundaries between these areas are somewhat fuzzy—one person's environment is another's input. Don't get too hung up on this. It doesn't matter how you categorize what you need to control, only that you successfully control it.

is to create an automated build process, something we'll discuss in more detail in Section 9.3, *Automatic Builds*, on page 147.

2.3 Controlling the Environment

What constitutes your software's environment depends on what kind of software it is. For traditional desktop software, the operating system is probably most relevant. For web software, it's the browser. For network software, it's the other software you're communicating with, and for embedded code, it's the hardware you're interfacing with.

Despite these differences, the key in all cases is first knowing what environment the bug manifests in. We'll discuss how to achieve that in Section 6.1, *Environment and Configuration Reporting*, on page 92. You then need convenient access to all the possible environments so that you can test in whichever is relevant.

Some of us are lucky enough to work in a development environment that is the same as (or similar enough to) the production environment. This means that we can probably reproduce problems easily on our development machine (and conversely, if everything works on our development machine, we can be pretty sure that it will work when deployed). But if you're targeting multiple platforms, writing embedded software, or developing on a laptop but hosting on a server, then you're going to have to find some way to replicate a production environment.

Reproducing different environments used to be a logistical nightmare— it wasn't unusual for software development houses to have entire rooms filled from floor to ceiling with different makes and models of computers so that every variation of hardware and operating system was available. Two things have helped immeasurably with this issue. The first is hardware abstraction—the days in which the graphics card in your computer might significantly affect your software's behavior are thankfully long gone.[3] The second is virtual machines—it's now possible to run many different operating systems and configurations on a single computer simultaneously, with very little effort indeed. This is of obvious use if you're working on cross-platform software, but it can also be helpful in a wide range of other circumstances.

If you're writing web software, for example, the chances are that you're going to need to support a wide range of different browsers, and prob-

---

3. Outside of a few specialist areas such as gaming, that is.

ably several different versions of each. The easiest way to achieve this (particularly given the difficulty of having multiple versions of some browsers installed on a single system) may be to have a number of different virtual machines available, each configured with a different operating system and browser combination.

Another example is if you're writing software that runs on a number of different computers simultaneously—maybe your software is deployed to a cluster of several machines? If so, you can create a "virtual data center" on a single development machine by running several virtual machines in parallel.

Finally, remember that the environment constitutes *anything* that might affect your software's behavior. Sometimes, as the following story shows, this can include some unlikely suspects.

> Your software's environment is anything that might affect its behavior.

It's the Pixies!

Dave was working on the device driver for a printer. After several weeks of work, he decided that it was ready and handed it off to our testing guys upstairs. Very quickly they found an intermittent bug in which spurious horizontal lines appeared in the output.

Try as hard as he might, Dave couldn't reproduce the problem. He printed page after page, with not a single failure. We started looking for differences between the test and development environments, but nothing we tried worked. This included shipping the entire test system downstairs. We picked up a system that reproduced the problem and carried it down a flight of stairs—after which it behaved itself perfectly.

This was the point when Dave suggested that the bug was caused by a clan of pixies who lived upstairs and got their kicks from interfering with printer innards. His theory turned out to be surprisingly close to the truth.

Our office was a very nice old stately home in the middle of the Cambridgeshire countryside. It was a lovely place to work, but it had its downsides. One of these downsides was that the wiring, although not quite as old as the building, *was* older than most of the people working in it. It turns out that the power upstairs wasn't very well conditioned, and these random fluctuations were enough to cause timing differences with the results we observed.

2.4 Controlling Inputs

Your software's inputs may be files on disc, sequences of user interface operations, or responses from third-party servers or hardware. Whatever form they take, the key is to first *identify* them so that you can then *replay* them exactly.

If you're lucky, the relevant inputs will be specified in the bug report, but this isn't always the case. It may be obvious to you that a bug report needs to enumerate every step involved, but your customers are unlikely to realize the importance of doing so. Or they may allow their preconceptions about how the software works (which may bear very little resemblance to what really goes on under the hood) to color their description.

Even if the user has conscientiously reported everything they did, it still may not be enough. Often the important details simply aren't obvious or even available to the end user. The bug might depend upon subtleties of timing, for example, or receiving certain input from a third-party system behind the scenes.

If you don't have all the information you need, you have two choices. You can either *infer* what the inputs might be or *record* them.

Inferring Inputs

The starting point for inferring the right inputs to reproduce the problem is to assume that the problem really does exist and then reverse engineer the necessary conditions that would lead to that behavior.

Work Backward

Often we know what has happened, but it's not obvious why it has happened.

For example, imagine that we have a bug report that specifies that the application crashed with a null dereference. We know which line of source code the null dereference occurred on from the error message, but we don't know what sequence of actions led to this point.

What we can do is work backward. We can infer that if variable a is null there, then that must mean that a nonexistent item identifier was passed to method $b()$, which in turn means that action c must have been invoked with a particular kind of input. . . .

If you are lucky, this kind of logic will lead directly to a reproduction. Even if it's not entirely conclusive, however, it can still provide clues that can be used together with additional evidence to eliminate possibilities.

Explore the Landscape

Even if the sequence of inputs in the bug report don't reproduce the problem, there's an excellent chance that something close to them will. Perhaps some vital step is missing, or they said they clicked *that* button when in reality it was *this* one. In that case, you can find the right sequence by exploring those that are similar to what's been reported.

Many of the techniques you're familiar with from testing will serve you well here, in particular boundary value analysis and branch coverage:

Boundary value analysis:

> Experience shows that the boundaries between input ranges are where errors are most likely to show up. If your software should do one thing when given a number up to 10 and do another thing when given 11 or more, then there's an excellent chance that giving it 10 or 11 will show up bugs. Other common boundary conditions are zero-length inputs or the point at which something changes from positive to negative.

Branch coverage:

> Branch coverage is the white-box equivalent of boundary value analysis (a black-box technique).[4] If you're unable to reproduce a problem with a particular sequence of inputs, try creating inputs that exercise different code branches in the same area.

Effectively identifying input sequences that reproduce a problem can require a shift of mental gears—you're not trying to prove that the system works; you're trying to prove that it's *broken*.

There Are *Other* Directions?

In *The Pragmatic Programmer* [HT00], Andy Hunt tells the story of a colleague who was struggling to reproduce a problem in a graphics application. The bug report said that the software crashed whenever a stroke was drawn with a particular brush, but he insisted that everything worked just fine.

---

4. *Black-box* techniques derive test cases without knowledge of the internals of the system under test. *White-box* techniques, by contrast, make use of our knowledge of how the system itself is constructed to create test cases.

After several days and with tempers fraying, they eventually worked out that whenever he "tested" the brush, he always drew a stroke from bottom left to top right (in other words, increasing both x- and y-coordinates). As soon as he tried a stroke in another direction, the application misbehaved on cue.

Force Error Conditions

It's human nature to focus on the "happy path" when writing code. We have a particular goal in mind and tend to concentrate on achieving it, without worrying about all the ways in which things could go wrong along the way. Couple that with the fact that testing error conditions can be tricky, and the result is that error conditions can be a rich source of bugs.

When trying to reproduce a problem, consider whether there's some error condition that could manifest somewhere in the middle of the process, and explain why the problem occurred. Then work out how you can either force that error condition to manifest or simulate it, and see whether that gives you your reproduction.

Introduce Randomness

One way to explore a range of different inputs is to introduce some random variability into the equation. If you're looking for a bug that seems to depend upon the exact details of timing, then introducing random variations into that timing is likely to increase the chances of the bug manifesting, for example.

Fuzz testing involves providing random data (fuzz) to a program, and a *fuzzer* automates the process (see Section A.4, *Testing Tools*, on page 200). Fuzzers create fuzz data through either *generation* or *mutation*:

Generation: Generational fuzzers build input based upon a data model, either from scratch or by combining existing data in interesting ways. This data model encodes an understanding of the software being tested in order to increase the chance of discovering problems.

Mutation: Mutating fuzzers start from a known-good template that is then modified according to a set of rules. Again, these rules are constructed in such a way as to increase the chance of the resulting input uncovering problems.

A crucial feature of all fuzzers is that they can re-create any of the input they generate so that if a problem does come to light, it can be reproduced at will.

When working through the process of inferring the inputs necessary to reproduce a problem, keep in mind that you need to verify your conclusions against the bug report. Just because you've found *a* way to cause the software to misbehave doesn't mean that you've found the one that the bug report is referring to (although you clearly have found a bug that you should fix).

Recording Inputs

An alternative to trying to infer the right inputs to reproduce the problem is to directly record them through *logging*. If your software already has built-in logging, this may simply be a case of asking the user to switch it on and send you the results. Alternatively, you may have to ship them a custom build of the software or some other logging solution (such as a debugging shim or proxy). Whichever solution you decide to use, seeing exactly what the user is really doing can be worth its weight in gold.

Logging

At its simplest level, capturing logging is simply a question of strategically placing calls to System.out.println() or similar throughout the code. And indeed this simplistic approach might be all you need. If your logging requirements are at all complex, however, you should consider using one of the many logging frameworks available (see Section A.3, *Logging*, on page 199).

A logging framework provides you with a great deal of useful functionality for free:

- The ability to switch logging on or off in particular areas as needed.

- Different log levels, allowing you to fine-tune the amount of logging generated. During normal operation, maybe you record only those occasions where the software hit a fatal error or just the headlines of what the software is up to without any of the detail. But when you need to, you can increase it to generate more detail, perhaps even to the extent of creating a detailed trace of exactly which functions were called when and with what parameters.

- Log messages that can be decorated with useful information such as which log level or module the message is associated with or even the exact source file line number.

- Standard tools to help analyze log files.

- Automatic logging of certain events, like unhandled exceptions.

What does using a logging framework look like in practice? Here's an example of a Java class that uses the java.util.logging framework:

```java
import java.util.logging.Logger;

public class Dispatcher {
❶    private static final Logger log = Logger.getLogger(Dispatcher.class.getName());

    public static void dispatchLoop() {
      while(true) {
        try {
          long start = System.currentTimeMillis();

          Item item = WorkQueue.getNextItem();
❷          log.fine("Processing item: " + item);
          item.process();

          long timeInMillis = System.currentTimeMillis() - start;
❸          log.info("Processing " + item + " took " + timeInMillis + "ms");
        } catch(Exception e) {
❹          log.severe("Unhandled exception: " + e);
        }
      }
    }
}
```

At ❶, we create a Logger instance, passing it the name of our class. Not only does this automatically annotate our log messages with the class name, but it also enables us to control messages generated here independently of other logging elsewhere. And then at ❷, ❸, and ❹, we generate messages at different log levels (FINE, INFO, and SEVERE, respectively). Which of these is actually output will depend on how we have things configured—perhaps normally we output only messages at level WARNING and above, but when we're trying to debug a problem, we reduce that level to FINEST?

Although we've been discussing logging in the context of accurately identifying the inputs used to reproduce a problem, it can be helpful in a wide range of other circumstances, as the following story shows.

Joe Asks...
Should I Leave My Logging in the Code?

Some topics are guaranteed to create an argument among developers, and logging is one of them.

If you've added logging to the code to help while tracking down a problem, it's tempting to leave this instrumentation in place so that you can find the problem again quickly if it happens again. This is especially true if you're using a logging framework that allows it to be enabled and disabled easily. What's not to like?

So, why the controversy? Detractors will tell you the following:

- Logging obscures the code, making it difficult to see the wood for the trees.

- Logging can suffer from the same problems as comments—as the code evolves, often the logging isn't updated to match, meaning that you can't trust what it says and making it worse than useless.

- No matter how much logging you add, it's never what you need. The next time you find yourself debugging in that area, you'll just have to add more, and if you leave it in the code when you're done, you just exacerbate the first two problems.

As with most disputes of this nature, the answer is to be pragmatic. Logging is a useful tool, but it can be overused. Consider implementing permanent logging if you believe that it will add value, but be disciplined about how you do so. Make sure that your logging is up-to-date and agrees with the code and that you don't add it for its own sake.

As a general rule, the most useful logging is at the highest (strategic) level—a record of what happened, such as the access log generated by an HTTP server, for example. Lower-level, more tactical logging can be of questionable long-term value, so make sure you know what it's giving you before you decide to add it.

If you find that logging is getting in the way but you don't want to lose its benefits, you might want to look at *aspect-oriented programming*, which may give you a way to separate it from the main body of the code (a good reference is *AspectJ in Action* (Lad03)).

The Ticking Time Bomb

While I was writing this chapter, we experienced a hardware failure on the server cluster hosting one of our applications—a SAN system suddenly marked all its drives as bad. We were fairly sure that the problem wasn't that all the drives had simultaneously failed, so clearly there was a problem with the SAN system itself.

Happily, the system in question kept a log, which the vendor was able to use to identify a timing window that arose once every 49.7 days. Within three days of the outage, they had diagnosed the problem and implemented a patch. Without the logging, all they would have had to go on was a mysterious failure. They would have had to spend a great deal of time trying to reproduce it (at least 49 days until the window opened again, and probably longer, because there was no guarantee that it would happen even then). By capturing key details of the inputs being received by the system and its internal state, they were able to short-circuit this whole process and implement and install a fix long before our system became vulnerable for a second time.

External Logging

Adding logging directly into the software isn't your only choice. You can also obtain a great deal of useful information from outside the software by intercepting traffic between it and elsewhere.

If, for example, your software communicates with another system over the network, you can insert a *proxy* in between the two systems, as shown in Figure 2.1, on the facing page. If a proxy doesn't exist for the protocol that you're using or you can't find a way to configure things so that the proxy can intercept traffic, you can consider using a network analyzer to capture all network traffic. You can find pointers to both of these tools in Section A.4, *Other Tools*, on page 200.

This approach isn't restricted to network communication. If your software communicates with a third-party library through an API, you might be able to intercept this communication by creating a *shim* that sits between your software and the library.[5] The shim links to the library and exports an identical API, forwarding all calls verbatim while logging.

---

5. In engineering, a shim is a thin piece of material used to fill the space between objects. In computing we've borrowed the term to mean a small library that sits between a larger library and its client code. It can be used to convert one API to another or, as in the case we're discussing here, to add a small amount of functionality without having to modify the main library itself.

Production:

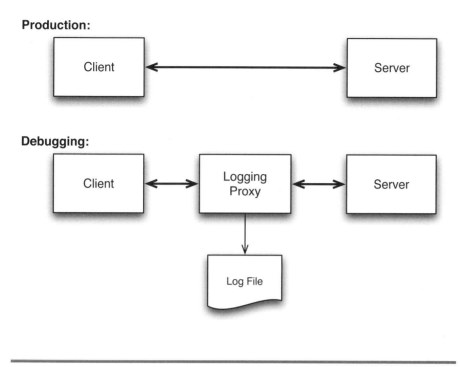

Debugging:

Figure 2.1: LOGGING PROXY

You might also find that the systems you're integrating with already provide more than enough support in this area. If you're writing a web application, for example, your application server will almost certainly already implement detailed and comprehensive logging.

Load and Stress

Some bugs manifest only when the software is under some kind of stress. This may be because of what the software itself is having to do (handle a large number of simultaneous requests, for example, or particularly large data sets). Or it may be because of something within the environment (high levels of general network traffic, say, or restricted free memory).

For obvious reasons, it can be difficult to reproduce this kind of load to debug such a problem—not many of us have testing departments with thousands of people on standby to replicate periods of heavy use.

A load-test tool executes a script that simulates a more-or-less realistic usage pattern. It can be configured to create as many concurrent sessions (possibly running on multiple client machines if a single client doesn't suffice) as you need to replicate whatever level of load you need.[6]

The issue with load-test tools is normally finding a way to get them to duplicate realistic load. It's easy to create a large number of simple interactions, but that may not generate load that is realistic enough to replicate the problem you're trying to debug. One way to address this is to use logging to record real usage and then use your load testing tool to replay it.

Stress-testing tools are similar, except they generate load indirectly. You might use one to allocate and deallocate lots of memory while your software is running, for example, or to consume lots of CPU time.

You can find pointers to some popular load testing tools in Section A.4, *Testing Tools*, on page 200.

Reproducing the problem once is an important hurdle—there's now no doubt that you're chasing a real bug, and you've made a significant step on the path to diagnosis. But there are helpful and less helpful ways to reproduce the bug. In the next section, we'll look at how to refine your reproduction and make it as effective as possible.

2.5 Refining Your Reproduction

Any means of reproducing the problem at all is better than none. But you're aiming for a reproduction that is both *reliable* and *convenient*. You're going to have to use it over and over again during diagnosis, so you need to be able to do so on demand and with minimal effort.

Minimizing the Feedback Loop

When running experiments to track your bug down, it's important that these experiments are as efficient as possible. A completely reliable reproduction that takes more than an hour to run, or requires you to perform 50 different actions in the right sequence, is not efficient.

---

6. The recent availability of *cloud computing* platforms, of which Amazon's Elastic Compute Cloud (EC2) is probably the best known, has made access to a large number of clients for load and stress testing much more convenient than it used to be.

What you're aiming for is the shortest and least error-prone edit-compile-execute-reproduce cycle you can create. You want to be able to run lots of experiments quickly so that you can understand all aspects of the problem

You want to be able to run lots of experiments quickly.

(and eventually test possible solutions) as thoroughly as possible.

As with so many other areas of software development, it's all about minimizing the feedback loop. The shorter the loop, the more timely and relevant the feedback.

In the absence of a short cycle, there is a real danger that you will find yourself tempted to make several changes at a time—as we will see when we come to discuss diagnosis, multiple simultaneous changes lead to all sorts of problems.

As Simple as Possible

It's unlikely that the first reproduction you discover will be minimal. In other words, it's probably more complicated than it needs to be. Your first concern, therefore, is to find out

Aim for a minimal reproduction.

which aspects of the reproduction are unnecessary and can be discarded.

For example, imagine that your software reads XML files, and you've determined that it crashes when reading a particular file containing 100 tags. There's an excellent chance that you don't need to read the entire file to reproduce the problem. If it crashes on one particular tag, perhaps you need a file containing just that single tag? Or just the few tags surrounding it?

It may not be that simple—there may be something earlier in the file that sets up the right context or that tag to subsequently invoke the bug. Nevertheless, you may find that large swathes of the file can be deleted.

Your intuition is often a good guide to which elements of a reproduction can be discarded. You understand your software and know which modules are likely to be affected by a particular piece of input and which aren't. If intuition fails, however, less direct approaches can be surprisingly effective.

Imagine that you're faced with a 100-line input file and it's not clear which line of the file invokes the bug. Try simply deleting the last half

Automatically Minimizing Input

It turns out that minimizing the input required to reproduce a bug can be automated. Andreas Zeller discusses one way of achieving this (by automating a binary chop) in *Beautiful Code: Leading Programmers Explain How They Think* (OW07).

Personally speaking, I've never seen this kind of approach used in the wild, but it is very cute. And perhaps it points to a fertile area for future tool support?

of the file, and see whether it still reproduces the problem. If it does, you've restricted the problem to the first half. If not, try deleting the first half; you may find that the second still invokes the bug. A few iterations of this, and you can quickly reduce the file to a handful of lines. The same approach can be applied to any kind of input (actions performed via the UI, responses from hardware, and so on).

This approach is one particular instance of *binary chop*, a search algorithm that turns out to be very useful in a wide range of debugging scenarios. We'll talk about it further in Section 3.2, *Divide and Conquer*, on page 48.

Youthful Exuberance

In between my degree and PhD research, I was lucky enough to be able to spend a summer internship at Microsoft within the compilers and tools team. I was working on the CodeView debugger and in the process discovered a bug in the then-unreleased version of the C compiler.

Thinking that I was being conscientious and helpful, I submitted a bug report in which I included the complete preprocessed output of the source file (several thousand lines by the time all of the #include directives had been processed).

A week or so later, the bug was closed as a duplicate, with a terse message from the developer who'd worked on it saying that after he'd whittled the several thousand lines down to the essential ten, it was obviously a duplicate of a bug that had been reported a few weeks earlier. A little more effort from me to make sure that my report was minimal would allowed me to have spotted the duplicate and save a colleague, with little spare time, a lot of work.

Don't get too disheartened if you can't find a means of minimizing your reproduction. Sometimes it really is irreducible, and on other occasions even though it could be simplified, you need to gain some insight into the problem before you can do so. As we'll discuss later, refining your reproduction isn't a one-time-only thing but something to keep in mind throughout diagnosis.

Minimize the Time Required

Some bugs just take time to reproduce—it's not what you do so much as how long you do it for. An example might be a web app that crashes after handling a few thousand requests. More often than not, this kind of problem turns out to be a resource leak of some variety (memory, file handles, or similar).

If you suspect this might be what's up, there are several approaches you might take to make it happen earlier. Most obviously, you can restrict the quantity of whatever resource is running out, either directly or by modifying the code to allocate a fair chunk of it during startup so that there's less left during normal operation. Alternatively, you can fake the resource running out, perhaps by replacing the function that allocates it with one that pretends to fail at the appropriate point.

Make Nondeterministic Bugs Deterministic

Part of the beauty of software is that it's deterministic—the computer does exactly what you tell it to do, and, given the same starting point, it will do exactly the same thing every time. Nevertheless, anyone who has developed software for any length of time will have come across nondeterministic software where—as far as you can tell—you do the same thing every time, but sometimes it behaves in one way, and sometimes another.

So, where does this nondeterminism come from? Well, it certainly isn't cosmic rays flipping bits at random (no matter how many old programmers' tales you hear). Nondeterminism can have only a few causes:

> Nondeterminism can have only a few causes.

- Starting from an unpredictable initial state
- Interaction with external systems
- Deliberate randomness
- Multithreading

We'll consider each of these in turn.

Joe Asks...

Why Are Nondeterministic Bugs a Problem?

Imagine that you are dealing with a bug that you can reproduce only every other time you try. You think that you've just implemented a fix. But because your reproduction is intermittent, you can't simply test your fix and infer that if the bug doesn't manifest, then it's good, because it might be simple chance that the bug didn't occur that time. Each time you try, you increase your confidence, but you can never be completely certain that you've fixed it.

If working out whether you've fixed an intermittent bug is difficult, then diagnosing one is even worse. Every time you run an experiment, you're not sure whether you're observing a run that is going to fail or one that isn't. This makes it very difficult to make progress. It's incredibly easy to get confused, draw broken inferences, and reach erroneous conclusions. On top of which, it's just plain frustrating!

Starting from an Unpredictable Initial State

This is normally a problem only if your software reads from uninitialized memory. Modern operating systems that always initialize memory before making it available, and modern languages that make it impossible to use memory without initializing it first, mean that this is a much less important source of nondeterminism than it used to be. C/C++ programmers running in certain environments will still have to worry about this, however. And even if your code is written in Java, you may well find yourself interfacing with third-party systems that have this issue, so you can't ignore it entirely.

If you have reason to believe that this might be the source of your nondeterminism, your best bet is probably using a debugging memory allocator (see Section A.3, *Debugging Memory Allocators*, on page 198) to force memory to be initialized to a well-known value, or a memory integrity checker (see Section A.4, *Runtime Analysis Tools*, on page 201) to detect references to uninitialized memory.

Interaction with External Systems

Often nondeterminism arising from interaction with an external system doesn't arise because it does something differently but because of subtleties of timing. Because it isn't running in lock-step with your software, sometimes its input will arrive when your software is in one state and sometimes when it's in another.

If you're faced with this issue, the trick is to control exactly what arrives from the external system and when. To this end, your best bet is probably not trying to control the external system directly but to replace it with something that you can control, such as a debugging subsystem or a test double (we'll discuss test doubles in Section 9.1, *Mocks, Stubs, and Other Test Doubles*, on page 141).

Deliberate Randomness

Randomness forms an intrinsic element of some software—games that deal cards, for example, or security software that generates random keys. It should come as no surprise that software that deliberately incorporates randomness behaves nondeterministically.

Luckily, most so-called random numbers used by software aren't really random at all but instead are *pseudo-random* numbers generated by a deterministic algorithm that does a good job of appearing to be random. They have the very useful property that if you set the *seed* (a value used to initialize the random number generator) to a known value, you'll always get the same sequence of numbers from the random number generator (and, therefore, completely predictable behavior).

Multithreading

Nondeterminism arising from multithreading can be especially difficult to deal with. On a single CPU, one thread can interrupt another at just about any point, and in these days of multicore systems, more often than not we're dealing with genuine concurrency.

If it's possible and you can still reproduce the problem that way, the simplest solution is often to run the software without any threading at all. If not, then you need to think about ways to force the software to context switch under your control, rather than at the whim of the scheduler. How easy this will be depends on how your software is designed and whether you've built such control in.

In the absence of a structured means of controlling concurrency, you're going to have to fall back on a more ad hoc approach. To that end, one of the most useful tools at your disposal is the humble sleep() method, which allows you to force a thread to wait long enough to force a *race condition* (behavior that depends critically upon the precise sequence or timing of events) to occur.

For example, imagine that you're working on software in which multiple worker threads process work items in parallel (a common pattern in multithreaded software). Workers obtain work items with the following Java code:

```java
if(item = workQueue.lockWorkItem()) {
  item.process();
  workQueue.writeResultAndUnlock(item);
}
```

You are trying to track down an intermittent bug in which it appears that occasionally the same work item is given to two workers simultaneously. Unfortunately, it happens only rarely. You can increase the chance of reproducing the problem by modifying the code as follows:

```java
if(item = workQueue.lockWorkItem()) {
❶  Thread.sleep(1000);
  item.process();
  workQueue.writeResultAndUnlock(item);
}
```

The call to sleep() at ❶ greatly enlarges the window during which the race condition can occur, making it much more likely to happen.

Note that although sleep() can be useful during reproduction or diagnosis, it is almost never the right tool to use when fixing a bug. We'll look at this in more depth in Section 8.3, *Concurrency*, on page 123.

Automate

Automating the steps necessary to reproduce a bug both speeds the process up and decreases the chance of making a mistake. The more complicated the reproduction, the greater the benefit, but it's worth considering even for relatively simple cases.

Automating with Tests

Perhaps the most fruitful avenue to explore is your automated test framework (assuming that you have one). A custom test is not only convenient to run but can also be an excellent starting point for the tests that you're going to end up writing when diagnosis is over and you start working on the fix.

Record:

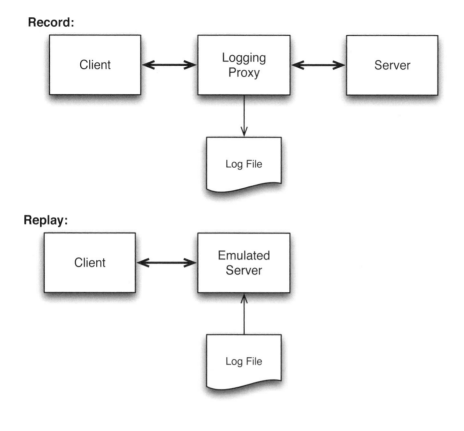

Replay:

Figure 2.2: REPLAYING FROM A LOG FILE

Alternatively, if your reproduction requires a long sequence of user interface actions, you might consider using one of the user interface test tools referenced in Section A.4, *Testing Tools*, on page 200.

Replaying Log Files

If you've identified your reproduction via logging, then you have another option—replaying the log file. In Figure 2.1, on page 25, we showed how a logging proxy can be used to record the interactions between the software you're trying to debug and a third-party server. In Figure 2.2, we can see that an emulated version of the third-party server, which reads from that log, can be used to re-create the same sequence of operations at will.

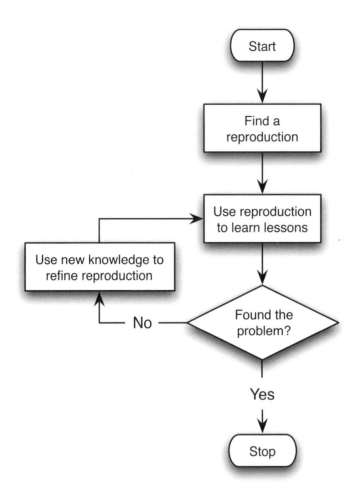

Figure 2.3: REFINING YOUR REPRODUCTION

Iterate

As you work your way through diagnosis, you build up more and more information about how and why the software is behaving as it is. You can and should use this information to continually refine your reproduction, as shown in Figure 2.3.

Imagine, for example, that you initially reproduce the problem by providing a large input file to your application. Your initial attempts to minimize the size of this file were unsuccessful, and (even worse) the bug occurs only one time in three. You might iteratively refine your reproduction as follows:

1. You determine that one particular module is involved, which allows you to pinpoint a particular element of the file that invokes the bug. This allows you to create a much smaller file.

2. As your diagnosis proceeds, you discover that you can force the problem to occur every time by replacing a subsystem that communicates with a third-party server with a stub that simply returns a canned response.

3. Finally, you track the problem down to a particular function and create a unit test that reproduces it by calling that function with a specific set of arguments.

Part of the art of good debugging is to always be on the lookout for opportunities to make life simpler for yourself like this.

2.6 What If You Really Can't Reproduce It?

Occasionally, no matter how hard you try, you simply find yourself unable to reproduce the bug you're chasing. So, what to do?

Does It Really Exist?

One possibility, of course, is that you're chasing a chimera and the bug doesn't really exist. If you have good evidence to support this, fine. But be careful that you really have exhausted all the avenues available to you—in my experience, we software developers tend to reach this conclusion too readily.

If you do decide to close the bug as "needs more info" or "works for me" (or whatever the equivalent status is in your bug-tracking system), don't simply stop there. Users don't (normally) report bugs maliciously. There's a good chance that something has gone wrong for them. Perhaps they haven't explained it as clearly as they might have done or have misunderstood some aspect of the software. Take the time to describe what you have done and identify any additional information that might help you get to the bottom of what they're really experiencing.

Work on a Different Problem in the Same Area

Are there any other bugs that you can reproduce in the same area? If so, even if they aren't (on the face of things) as serious or as urgent as the one you're currently chasing, it might be worth attacking them instead. There are two reasons why this might help.

First, this can be a good way to tidy up the code in the area. You may find that the problem you were really looking for was being masked by other issues. Get them out of the way, and you can see what you were originally looking for more clearly.

Second, working on a problem that you can reproduce is an excellent way of gaining a better understanding of the code in general. There's an excellent chance that this increased understanding will provide some insight that will enable you to find the key to reproducing the problem you originally started looking for.

And even if none of this helps, the worst that happens is that you end up fixing a few less urgent bugs.

Get Others Involved

We developers can easily develop blind spots. We necessarily have a different perspective from our users, and that can mean we miss important information that would be obvious to someone who understands things from their point of view. Furthermore, our focus tends to be on working out how to make the software work, not proving that it's broken.

To that end, it can help to bring in someone who can attack the problem from an alternative direction. Your customer support team, for example, is likely to have a good understanding of your users. And your test team's entire *raison d'être* is finding ways to prove that the software is broken.

If you can, the best person to talk to is whoever reported the bug in the first place. We'll discuss this further in Section 6.2, *Working with Users*, on page 94.

Leverage Your User Community

If the bug manifests in the wild but not in your development system, you might be able to get your users to gather the information you need. This is far from an ideal situation because:

- You'll need to find some way to get instrumented versions of the software to these users.

- It works only with some user communities—they will need to be prepared to go to some trouble to help you out and may need to be reasonably technically competent.

- The iteration length, from you deciding what information you need to gather to receiving it back from the field, is much longer than you would prefer.

But if your situation allows you to consider this, it can be very effective. This approach is particularly worthwhile if you're working on open source software because open source user communities can be much more open to participating in the debugging process.

Dead Reckoning

Although the empirical approach to debugging is normally the best, it certainly isn't the only way to proceed. If you can't reproduce the bug, then a crucial tool that enables empirical debugging is missing, and you have to explore other avenues.

One such avenue is purely logical proof of why the software is behaving as it is. This is likely to be very time-consuming and may prove intractable. But it can work where other approaches have failed.

What you're aiming to do is to "think yourself into the software," executing it in your imagination. At each step, think about what could go wrong, which might explain the bug you're trying to track down.

Replication Woes

We were working on a web application sitting on top of a MySQL database. MySQL provides a very useful replication feature, which we were using to configure two servers into a master and a slave. The master did all the work, while the slave replicated everything happening on the master. This meant that it could be used as a hot spare if the master failed. Life was good.

Most of the time.

Every once in a while the slave would crash with a very obscure error message. The only way that we could resurrect the system was to re-create the slave's copy of the master database and reconfigure replication from scratch. Sometimes the slave would crash within a few days of restarting replication, and sometimes it would run for months without a problem.

Clearly something was wrong, but we had no idea what it might be. We eliminated hardware as a possible cause, because we could swap the master and slave, and it was still the machine that was acting as the slave that failed. We couldn't replicate the problem in a test system—it occurred only on the production servers, and none of the logging we put in place gave us any insight into what was happening.

We feared that the only way that we'd be able to reproduce it would be to buy two more servers for testing and write a very complicated test harness that would simulate realistic load. Clearly this was going to be a long, involved, and expensive bug to track down.

Before doing so, however, I decided to go over the scripts we were using to create the replication relationship in detail. I sat down with a printout of them, a copy of the MySQL documentation, and everything that I could find via Google about ways in which MySQL replication could go wrong. After a day of crawling through the scripts, drawing diagrams on the whiteboard, and acting out possible scenarios with other members of the team ("I'm the master, you're the slave, and Thomas is going to be a client—what happens when...?"), we eventually detected a race condition in the locking we used to ensure that we got a consistent snapshot of the database.

Having identified it, the fix was easy, and the slave has replicated perfectly ever since.

Happily, situations such as the previous are very rare—normally you will be able to reproduce the problem. In the next chapter, we'll look at how to use that reproduction to reach a diagnosis.

2.7 Put It in Action

- Find a reproduction before doing anything else.
- Ensure that you're running the same version as the bug was reported against.
- Duplicate the environment that the bug was reported in.
- Determine the input necessary to reproduce the bug by:
    - Inference
    - Recording appropriate inputs via logging
- Ensure that your reproduction is both *reliable* and *convenient* through iterative refinement:
    - Reduce the number of steps, amount of data, or time required.
    - Remove nondeterminism.
    - Automate.

Chapter 3

Diagnose

Diagnosis is *the* key element of debugging. This is where the rubber meets the road and you arrive at the understanding of the root cause of the behavior you're seeing.

In this chapter, we will cover the following:

- The core diagnostic process

- Different types of experiment and what makes a good experiment

- Useful stratagems

3.1 Stand Back—I'm Going to Try Science

Although you're going to be using various tools and techniques and leveraging your software itself to help you, your primary asset is and always will be your intellect. Diagnosis takes place within your mind, not within your computer.

The mind-set you need to cultivate when debugging is similar (because the problem is similar) to that of a detective solving a crime or a scientist investigating a new phenomenon.

Balance creativity with rigor.

Open-minded at the same time as methodical, creative at the same time as thorough—as with so many other aspects of software development, effective bug fixing is all about finding the appropriate balance between these apparently contradictory demands.

The scientific method can work in two different directions.[1] In one case, we start with a hypothesis and attempt to create experiments, the results of which will either support or refute it. In the other, we start with an observation that doesn't fit with our current theory and as a result modify that theory or possibly even replace it with something completely different.

In debugging, we almost always start from the latter. Our theory (that the software behaves as we think it does) is disproved by an observation (the bug) that demonstrates that we are mistaken. In the words of Thomas Huxley, "The great tragedy of Science—the slaying of a beautiful hypothesis by an ugly fact."

A Debugging Method

Having discovered that things aren't as you believed them to be, your task is to modify your understanding of the software until you *do* understand what's really going on. To do that, you operate in the other of the two possible directions—create a hypothesis that might provide an explanation and then construct experiments to test it.

So, here's our idealized process (see Figure 3.1, on the next page):

1. Examine what you know about the software's behavior, and construct a hypothesis about what might cause it.

2. Design an experiment that will allow you to test its truth (or otherwise).

3. If the experiment disproves your hypothesis, come up with a new one, and start again.

4. If it supports your hypothesis, keep coming up with experiments until you have either disproved it or reached a high enough level of certainty to consider it proven.

That's all well and good but rather abstract. How do you translate this into action?

Different Types of Experiments

Your starting point is the reproduction we discussed at length in the previous chapter. From that starting point, you can run several types

---

1. Students of the history and philosophy of science will realize that I am skating over many subtleties.

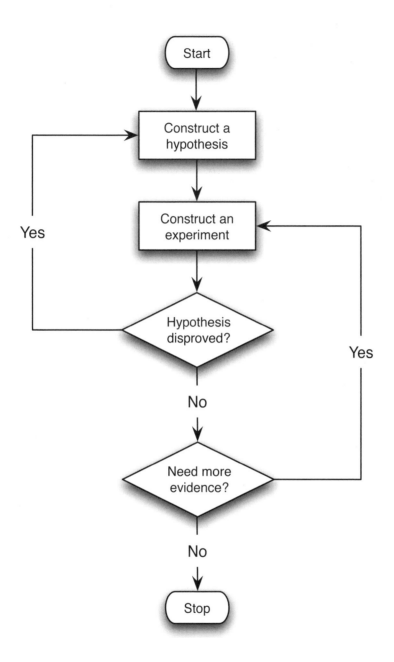

Figure 3.1: A DEBUGGING METHOD

of experiment—each of which involves changing one aspect of how you reproduce the problem:

- You can examine an aspect of the software's internal state (either by instrumenting it directly or by running it under a debugger).

- You can modify some aspect of how you run the software (modified inputs, for example, or an alternative environment) and see whether it behaves differently.

- You can change the logic encoded within the software itself and examine the effect of that change.

Which of these you choose depends upon the nature of your hypothesis, and making the best choice comes down to experience and intuition.

Whichever you choose, however, the most important thing to bear in mind is that your experiment must have a clear goal.

Experiments Must Prove Something

Experiments are a means to an end, not an end in themselves. There is no point performing an experiment unless it proves something.

> **What is your experiment going to tell you?**

Before investing time and effort to construct and run an experiment, ask yourself what it's going to tell you. What are the possible outcomes? If none of those outcomes would move you closer to your diagnosis, you need to come up with a different experiment. Beware of confusing activity with progress—if an experiment cannot increase your understanding, it's a waste of your time.

You can design experiments that are intended to *prove* your hypothesis or to *disprove* it. It might seem counterintuitive, but frequently the latter are the more useful. In part, this is because it's difficult to incontrovertibly prove something (just because you see what you expect to see doesn't mean that you're seeing it for the reason you think you are), but mainly it's a question of psychology.

If you have a plausible explanation for what's happening, it's very easy to talk yourself into seeing what you want to see. Playing devil's advocate and trying to disprove your hypothesis can be very productive, helping you spot possible holes in the explanation that you wouldn't see otherwise. If, after you've tried your hardest to disprove it, it's still standing at the end, then you can have a lot of confidence that you've nailed it. And every once in a while you will surprise yourself and find that something very different from what you thought was happening.

One Change at a Time

One of the basic rules of constructing experiments is that you should make only a single change at a time.

If you make a single change and see an effect, you can be pretty certain that the one caused the other.[2] If you make more than one change, however, it can be very difficult to be sure which change resulted in which effect. Or the

> Multiple changes lead to misleading conclusions.

changes may interact in unpredictable ways. At best, this might mean that you are unable to conclude anything useful. At worst, you may reach misleading conclusions that lead you down completely the wrong path.

This rule applies to any kind of change—changes to the source, the environment, input files, and so on. It applies to anything, in fact, that might have an effect on the software.

For some reason, this principle is forgotten surprisingly frequently—I don't know how many times I've seen someone make several changes all at once and then try to make sense of the results afterward. Although it can seem as though you're saving yourself time by making several changes simultaneously, all that you really achieve is the risk of invalidating your results. Maintain your discipline, and avoid falling into this trap.

Finally, once you see a change in behavior, undo whatever apparently caused it, and verify that the behavior returns to what it was beforehand. This is a very powerful indication that you're looking at cause and effect rather than serendipity.

Keep a Record of What You've Tried

If you find yourself working on a bug that takes days or weeks to track down, you will end up carrying out many different experiments. Ideally, each one will eliminate a set of possible causes, and eventually you will zero in on the root cause.

---

2. Not completely certain—a changing underlying system can get in the way of this kind of reasoning, but it's an excellent starting hypothesis.

When the diagnosis goes on this long and involves this many experiments, there is a danger that you will lose track of what you've done. This may mean that you waste time investigating possibilities that have already been eliminated by previous experiments, or it could result in you heading down a blind alley. In the worst case, it could lead you to a broken conclusion and subsequent misdiagnosis.

Periodically review what you've already tried and learned.

The best defense is to maintain a record of the experiments you've tried and what the results were. This doesn't have to take a long time or include huge amounts of detail—just enough to ensure that you don't forget what you've already done. Periodically review your notes to refresh your memory and help you identify the most promising next steps.

Many developers find it helpful to maintain a *daybook*. They might use it to record notes from meetings, design sketches, a record of the steps necessary to install a piece of software—anything, in fact, that might prove useful to refer to in the future. A daybook can be an excellent place to record your experiments. Or alternatively, if you prefer to keep your notes electronically, you might consider keeping a personal wiki.

Ignore Nothing

Occasionally you will notice odd behavior. You run an experiment, expecting one of result A or result B, and instead get result C. Or you work through a set of instructions about how to reproduce the bug, and the software does something very different from what you expect.

It can sometimes be tempting to shrug it off as "one of those things" and try a different tack. Don't! The software is trying to tell you something, and it's in your interest to listen.

If something unexpected happens, it means that some assumption you're making is broken. This might be an assumption about how the software should behave, what the bug you're trying to hunt down is, how you've constructed your experiment, or anything else. If you have a broken assumption, then the most valuable thing that you can do is to stop, identify, and fix it. If you don't, then all bets are off, and you can't trust any conclusions you reach.

This kind of thing can turn out to be a blessing in disguise—a shortcut to what's really going on. Getting to the bottom of unexpected behavior can save you a huge amount of wasted time chasing will-o'-the-wisps.

\/\/ Joe Asks...

How Else Can a Daybook Help When Debugging?

As well as maintaining a record of your experiments, a daybook can also be useful for the following:

- Writing out hypotheses. Getting things onto paper can help identify flaws in assumptions, especially when the hypothesis is complex.

- Keeping track of details such as stack traces, argument values, and variable names. Not only does this help with finding things again, but it also helps you communicate with colleagues when explaining the problem, avoiding the need to rely upon memory.

- Keeping a list of ideas to try. Often you will notice something else you want to investigate, or a possible follow-up experiment will occur to you, but you don't want to abandon the current experiment to pursue it. A "to-do" list ensures that you don't forget to come back to it later.

- Doodling when you need to take your mind off the problem.

Even if the odd behavior you notice doesn't have any bearing on the problem at hand, the fact that you've discovered something unexpected is valuable. Anything that you don't understand is potentially a bug. Once you've

> Anything that you don't understand is potentially a bug.

demonstrated to your satisfaction that it isn't relevant to what you're working on, feel free to put it aside, but don't forget about it. Keep a record (file a bug report perhaps) and come back to it. Often things discovered in passing like this prove to be real issues that need fixing. And you would much rather fix them having discovered them this way than wait until they're reported by an irate customer.

Sneaky!

I was crawling through yesterday's server log file gathering evidence that would help me diagnose the problem I was working on. In passing, I noticed that one of our users seemed to be having connection problems—he was logging out and then back in over and over again.

This had nothing whatsoever to do with the problem I was chasing, and I very nearly let it pass. Connection problems aren't that unusual, after all. But something didn't feel right—the pattern was too regular. My "spidey sense" was tingling.

Sure enough, it turns out that the user in question had found a sneaky way to bypass one of the security mechanisms implemented by the software (which rationed how much of a certain resource each user could consume). By logging out and then immediately back in again, he could reset his quota. It was an easy bug to fix now that we knew about it.

3.2 Stratagems

Although every bug is different, certain techniques and approaches have repeatedly proven their value in tracking down a wide range of problems. They won't suffice for every problem you find yourself faced with, but every programmer should have them at their fingertips.

Instrumentation

Diagnosis is all about information—divining precisely the state of, and the execution path taken by, the software. Although there are many ways through which you can either infer or derive this information, by far the simplest and most direct is adding *instrumentation* to the software itself.

Instrumentation is code that doesn't affect how the software behaves but instead provides insight into why it behaves as it does. In the previous chapter, we already discussed the most common and important type of instrumentation, logging. Possibly the oldest debugging technique is adding ad hoc logging to the code[3] in order to confirm or refute our beliefs about what it's doing.

The full facilities of the language are at your disposal.

Instrumentation isn't limited to simple output statements, however—you have the full facilities of the language at your disposal. You can collect and collate data, evaluate arbitrary code, and test for relevant conditions—the only limit is your imagination.

---

3. Often called printf() debugging after the C function of the same name.

> ### Beware of Heisenberg
>
> One of the lessons of quantum physics is that the act of observing a system can change the system itself. Computer software isn't quantum mechanical (not yet, anyway), but we still need to be wary.
>
> Instrumenting software intrinsically involves changing it, which raises the specter of affecting, instead of simply observing, its behavior. This is dangerous during diagnosis, because introducing an unintentional change during a series of experiments can easily lead to you draw invalid conclusions.
>
> Fundamentally speaking, there is no way that you can guarantee to avoid introducing *some* side effects. The fact that you've modified the source code means that the layout of the object code in memory and the timing of its execution will be affected. Happily, most of the time this remains a purely hypothetical problem—as long as you're careful to avoid the more obvious side effects, you can normally ignore the issue.
>
> Nevertheless, it is very good practice to keep the source code as close to its pristine form as possible. Don't allow failed experiments, along with their possible side effects, to accumulate over time. Keeping things neat also helps ensure that the code remains easy (or at least, no harder) to understand and will help ensure that you don't check in unintended changes when you eventually come to fixing the problem.

Let's look at an example. Imagine that you're trying to track down a bug in some Java code that traverses a data structure, processing each node in turn:

```java
while(node != null) {
  node.process();
  node = node.getNext();
}
```

You're seeing behavior that suggests that nodes are being processed more than once (in other words, getNext() is returning one or more nodes more than once). It's not clear which nodes are being processed more than once, however.

One way to find the problem would be to instrument the code as follows:

```
❶  HashSet processed = new HashSet();

   while(node != null) {
❷      if(!processed.add(node)) {
          System.out.println("The problem node is: " + node);
        }

        node.process();
        node = node.getNext();
   }
```

At ❶, we create a HashSet that we'll use to store the nodes that have already been processed. At ❷, we add the current node to the set. The add() method returns false if the object is already in the set, meaning that we've already processed this node.

Often, we create instrumentation like this on the fly and remove it once it has served its purpose. Instrumentation doesn't have to be temporary, however—there are good reasons why you might choose to leave it in the code, creating self-debugging software. We'll look at ways in which you can do so in Section 10.1, *Assumptions and Assertions*, on page 157.

Divide and Conquer

Divide and conquer, or *binary chop*, is the Swiss Army knife of debugging—it crops up again and again in a wide variety of situations.

Binary chop is a search strategy. Imagine, for example, that you have a sorted array of 1 million integers and are trying to identify whether a particular number appears within the array. You could simply examine each in turn but on average would expect to have to examine half of them before you found the one you were looking for. And in the worst case, you would have to examine all million.

Alternatively, you can find the midpoint of the array (dividing it into two halves, each of length 500,000). If the value at the end of the first half is less than the value you're looking for, then you know that you need to search only the second half. If not, you need to search only the first. Choose the relevant half, and divide it in half again (250,000 this time). Continue in this fashion, and you're guaranteed to find your target after twenty steps (in general, binary chop will require no more than log_2N steps where N is the number of items being searched).

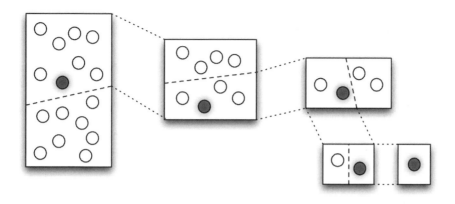

Figure 3.2: BINARY CHOP

The last few steps of this process are shown graphically in Figure 3.2.

We've already discussed one instance in which binary chop can help during debugging (in Section 2.5, *Refining Your Reproduction*, on page 26), but there are many others.

You may be tracking down a memory corruption. You have a means of detecting it (perhaps after the corruption, a variable that should be null is no longer) but don't know which of several thousand lines of code is causing it. Insert your check halfway through the suspect body of code, and reproduce your problem. If the check detects the corruption, then you can infer that the culprit lies somewhere in the first half of the code. If not, then the memory remained uncorrupted when your check executed, and the problem must lie somewhere in the second half. Rinse and repeat, and before long you will have identified the exact line of code.

Sometimes you won't be able to follow this approach all the way to a conclusion, but it can still provide you with a quick and easy way to exclude a large number of candidates. Perhaps your software contains a number of modules that can be enabled and disabled independently? If so, try disabling them all and see whether the bug still occurs. If it does, then you've eliminated a lot of code that you won't need to examine (and won't confuse matters). If it doesn't, then you can quickly identify the problem module by enabling half and rerunning your test.

Ultimately, this will allow you to narrow your search to only a single module, but that's still a considerable help.

Don't get too hung up on the binary aspect of this approach. Binary chop works most efficiently if you can divide your search space into approximately equal halves, but all you really need is some way to eliminate significant chunks of it at a time.

In the next section, we'll discuss how your source control system can help you find a regression. And guess what? It's yet another instance in which binary chop helps.

Leveraging Source Control

Occasionally, you will find yourself chasing a *regression*—a bug in functionality that used to work correctly but was broken by some subsequent change. Your normal diagnostic toolbox remains just as applicable to this kind of problem as any other, but there is one tool of particular value when regression hunting—your source control system.

If you can identify exactly which change introduced the problem, then diagnosing why it did so may be trivial. Your source control system maintains a complete history of every change that's ever been made to the software. All you need to do is identify exactly which one was the culprit.

The first step is to review check-in comments—it may be that the culprit is obvious. If not, however, you can quickly pinpoint the change using the following procedure.

Imagine that you know that the bug wasn't present in version 2.3, but it is present in the current version, 3.0. In between 2.3 and 3.0 are 200 different check-ins. You know the drill by now—check out and build the middle revision, and see whether the bug is present. If not, it was introduced by a more recent change; otherwise, it was one of the earlier ones. A few iterations later, and you know exactly which change it was.[4]

Sometimes you'll look at the change in question and be none the wiser. But it's not as if pinpointing the change could possibly hurt—at the very least, it's likely to eliminate a wide range of source code from your investigation.

---

4. This technique is so useful that the Git source control system provides direct support for it in the form of the git bisect command; see *Pragmatic Version Control Using Git* [Swi08] for more details.

Focus on the Differences

Your software normally works. So, the feature affected by the bug you're trying to diagnose probably works correctly in almost all situations or for almost everyone else. So, what you're looking for is something that makes this particular situation or customer special. You already know that part of the solution will be something that is unique to this one case—all you need to do is find out what it is.

Often these differences come to light when trying to reproduce the problem. Does it happen in only one particular environment? In that case, the problem is most likely in environment-specific code. Does it happen only with large input files? Most likely you're looking for a resource leak or a limit being exceeded.

If the differences didn't come to light during reproduction, it might prove helpful to "find the boundaries" of the bug. If you can identify several similar ways of running the software, some of which reproduce the problem and some of which don't, the chances are that it will teach you something.

Learn from Others

Many bugs will be completely specific to your own code, and therefore only you, or someone else on your team, will be able to address them. But sometimes the bug will relate to a widely used technology (your compiler, for example, or a library or framework you're using) in which case there's a chance that someone else has run afoul of the same problem before you.

In such instances, a little research on the Web can play dividends. Perhaps someone has asked a question about the same kind of failure module on a forum or has written a blog post describing the pitfall they fell into, which turns out to be exactly the one you find yourself in.

Occam's Razor

The oft-quoted Occam's Razor can be paraphrased as "All other things being equal, the simplest explanation is the best."

> All other things being equal, the simplest explanation is the best.

It's nothing more than a rule of thumb—any explanation that fits the facts could be the real one, including the most involved, convoluted, and implausible. But you have to pick one to explore first, and often it's the simple one that proves the most fruitful.

3.3 Debuggers

Debuggers vary dramatically in both sophistication and capabilities, from simple command line–oriented examples to those that are fully integrated into a graphical IDE. What they all have in common is that they allow us to examine the code as it executes, setting breakpoints, single-stepping, and examining program state.

It may seem odd that I've left discussing debuggers until this late in the chapter (and indeed, the book). For some developers, debugging *is* using a debugger—it's the first, and possibly only, tool that they reach for.

There's no doubt that your debugger is one of the most powerful tools in your toolbox, and you should certainly take the time to become familiar with what it can do and proficient in its use. But here's the thing—as time goes on, I find myself using the debugger less and less. And it seems that I'm not alone—many other developers I talk to tell me that they're finding the same thing. So, what's going on?

What has changed is test-first development (see Section 9.1, *Automated Testing*, on page 139). Where in the past my first instinct might have been to break out the debugger, now it's to write a test. To understand why, it helps to think about why we might use a debugger. It's particularly helpful at three different points of the development life cycle:

1. During initial development, it's helpful when single-stepping through code helps to convince us that what it's really doing agrees with what we thought we were implementing.

2. If we have a theory about why the code is behaving in a particular way, we can use the debugger to confirm or refute this theory.

3. Finally, a debugger helps us explore code that is behaving in a way we simply don't understand.

> Debugging sessions are ephemeral; tests are permanent.

But add test-first development into the equation, and the picture changes. Now, rather than stepping through the code to check that it behaves as we expect, we write one or more tests that demonstrate that it does. If we have a theory about what's causing a bug, we create a test that proves it. And the beauty of this is that unlike stepping through in a debugger, the results of which are ephemeral, a test is permanent. Not only does

The Interactive Console

If you're working in an interpreted language like Python or Ruby, another tool is available to you—the interactive console. This allows you to enter language statements directly and have them execute immediately, even redefining functions if the mood takes you. The console can be a wonderfully useful exploratory tool, either when debugging or when trying something new to see how it works.

If you're working in a compiled language, you may not be completely left out—some of the more sophisticated debuggers for compiled languages manage to provide something that comes very close to an interactive console. It's not quite the same thing, but it might be close enough.

it prove that the code works now, but it continues to do so in the future and can be run (and even improved) by other team members. Not only does it prove that our theory is correct, but we can subsequently use it to verify that our fix addresses the issue.

So, that leaves the debugger as an exploratory tool. It's a vital role to be sure, but it's a smaller one than it held a few years ago.

As an aside, this fact turns out to be very convenient if you're using a relatively new environment such as Ruby. The current Ruby debugger could charitably be described as "primitive," but that's much less of an issue than it might have been a few years ago, because the debugger is less of a crutch than it used to be.

3.4 Pitfalls

There are innumerable ways to trip up during diagnosis, but there are a few that crop up repeatedly. In this section, we'll look at some hard-won lessons from the trenches.

Are You Changing the Right Thing?

If the changes you're making have no effect, you're not changing what you think you are.

If the changes you're making don't seem to be having an effect, you're not changing what you think you are. Perhaps you're editing a file in one source tree but compiling a different one? Or you're compiling the right file but running the wrong executable? Or the code that you're editing is disabled by the preprocessor? Or your browser is pointing at the production server instead of the development server? Or. . . .

This pitfall is so common, so easy to fall into, and so confusing (until the eureka moment hits and you suddenly realize your mistake) that you will fall prey to it. The only defense is to always have the possibility at the back of your mind.

The easiest way to prove that you have succumbed can be to introduce deliberate, very obvious failures in the code. Perhaps an obvious syntax error or an #error directive if you're using C++? Or a call to System.exit()? When your compilation fails to break or your application stubbornly runs, it's time to search for your (now obvious) mistake.

Validate Your Assumptions

Everything you do is based upon a foundation of assumptions. You can't possibly avoid making them, and it's crazy to try—you can't work from first principles every time.

But assumptions are dangerous, because they create blind spots— things you treat as true without necessarily having direct evidence.

Some are less dangerous than others. Assuming that your compiler faithfully translates your source code into correct object code is probably safe, for example. Assuming that the method written by a colleague last week works exactly as intended maybe less so.

Know what assumptions you're making, and examine them critically.

The key is to understand what assumptions you're making, as well as when to examine them critically. A particularly good time to do so is when you're stuck—it may be because one of them is blinding you to what's really going on.

How Coherent Is Coherent?

Back in the early 90s, I was working on a performance-intensive, cross-platform application. It was already running successfully on several different shared-memory multiprocessor architectures, so when I was asked to port it to the then-new DEC Alpha, everyone expected that it would be a breeze. If only.

After weeks of crawling through thousand-line log files, I couldn't come up with any explanation of the behavior I was seeing. It was as though one CPU was seeing things written by another in a different order. But that couldn't possibly be true, could it?

Like just about every other machine of this type, the Alpha implemented *coherent caches* to guarantee that each CPU has a consistent view of shared memory. And we had assumed that "coherent" meant that writes to memory by one CPU would be seen by another in the order they were originally made.

In desperation, I created a tiny (less than twenty lines long) test program that spawned a couple of threads and screamed loudly if it ever saw reordered writes. And within seconds it was screaming. Coherent didn't mean what we thought it did—we needed to use *memory barriers* to guarantee ordering where it was important.[5]

Multiple Causes

Most commonly during diagnosis, you're looking for *the* cause of the problem, and normally, this is the right thing to do. As Occam's Razor tells us, simple explanations tend to be the most fruitful, and assuming that there's a single cause is much simpler than imagining several.

Nevertheless, as we've already seen, Occam's Razor is only a guide, and sometimes things really are complicated.

> Sometimes, things really are complicated.

The most common warning that you might face multiple causes is a feeling that you're in the twilight zone—weird things happening that seem to have no obvious explanation.

The most fruitful approach to multiple causes is to isolate the problems and find a way to reproduce a bug that depends upon one of the causes and not the other. How easy this will be depends upon how far through your diagnosis you've come. If you already have a good feeling

---

5. Nowadays we're all used to highly optimized CPUs that reorder things to improve performance, but it was a new one on us back then.

for where one of the problems may reside, that can help you construct an alternative reproduction that bypasses the other.

An alternative approach is to start by looking at any other bugs you might be aware of in the same area. Addressing these can sometimes clear things up or improve your understanding enough to throw your original problem into sharper relief.

If neither of these approaches works, then take a deep breath—this one is going to be a challenge. You're going to have to continue with your diagnosis as before, while bearing in mind that your experiments might behave unpredictably because they are being affected by more than one underlying issue. But then nobody said that debugging was easy.

Shifting Sands

Another cause of that "twilight zone" feeling is a changing underlying system. The rock upon which the empirical method we're relying upon depends is that we can reproduce the problem over and over again, obtaining the same results each and every time. Take that certainty away, and making progress becomes extremely difficult.

It's at times like this that the record you've been keeping (you have been keeping a record?) of what you've already tried and the results you obtained becomes worth its weight in gold. If you rerun an experiment that gave you one result yesterday and get a different result today, that's an excellent indication that something has changed in the interim.

If faced with a changing underlying system, stop and work out what's changing and why.

If you suspect that you might be suffering from this issue, stop immediately—forging ahead will just dig you into an even deeper hole. Your primary goal is identifying what, exactly, is changing so you can control it.

The most obvious candidates are things such as databases or third-party systems that the software interacts with, but remember that your software's behavior can be affected by a myriad different things. Perhaps you now have less free disk space and there's no longer room for a temporary file? Or you installed a new software package that updated a system library? Or if your software depends upon the time of day, it might even be reacting differently just because the time has changed?

What Do You Mean There Are *Twelve* Months?

One of my first experiences of working within a team was the group programming task we had to solve during my degree course. It was an education in more ways than one.

My team contained one member who was, frankly, useless. We threw all the code that he wrote (not that he wrote much) away with one exception—a function to return the number of days in a month.

Anyway, the code worked just fine, and we submitted it on time, passing all the tests. And then our professor contacted us to tell us that it crashed every single time it was executed. We very quickly tracked the problem down to the one function we hadn't rewritten, which looked like this:

```c
int days_in_month(int month) {
  switch(month) {
    case APRIL: return 30;
    case MAY: return 31;
  }
}
```

We submitted in May, but our professor didn't start his evaluation until June. Hey ho. . . .

3.5 Mind Games

Debugging is hard. On occasion, it's really hard. In the course of your career, you are guaranteed to hit situations where (for a while, at least) you simply can't see a way forward.

Sometimes it will seem as though what the software is doing is clearly impossible. Every piece of evidence contradicts what you're seeing. If it wasn't for the fact that it is happening, you would swear that it couldn't.

On other occasions, every avenue you investigate turns into a blind alley, and you simply can't think of anything else to try.

Don't be disheartened. Rest assured that we've all been there—and we all will be again. This is just part and parcel of developing software. You *will* find a way through eventually.

If you find yourself confronted by a roadblock, here are some techniques you might find helpful to break through it.

Cardboard Cutout Debugging

The single most powerful unblocking tactic at your disposal is to ask for help. Having a fresh pair of eyes examine the problem, someone

---

\\// Joe Asks...

What Makes a Good Cardboard Cutout?

Although the name suggests that a cardboard cutout would be just as effective, in fact the technique is much weaker if the helper isn't a living, breathing human being. Some people might be able to treat their cat as though it could really understand what they're saying, but most of us struggle to suspend disbelief.

This suggests that there are things that you can do when you're playing the cardboard cutout role to help:

- Pay attention. It will be obvious to the person you're "helping" if you're really balancing your checkbook in the back of your mind.

- Ask questions. Unclear aspects of the explanation are a warning flag; they are likely to contain unexamined assumptions.

- Keep an eye out for unexplored avenues. Don't assume that what's obvious to you is obvious to the person you're helping—they've asked you over because they're stuck, and often we get stuck on what seem to be trivialities.

- Do your best to understand what's going on. If you understand, you're likely to ask better questions. And it may be that lightning strikes you, not the person with the problem.

---

who hasn't been immersed in the problem for the last several hours (or days or weeks), can bring a new perspective. Even if they don't immediately spot the problem, two minds are better than one, and there's an excellent chance that between you, you'll work it out.

What's Going on Here?
by Jeremy J. Sydik

My two-year-old son, Aidan, caught a bug once. He started pointing at a screen of Lisp code that I'd been sorting through for fifteen to twenty minutes. He'd noticed that the indentation pattern didn't look like the others on the screen.

But, as anyone who's ever done this will know, often the simple act of explaining the problem is all it takes for inspiration to strike. Some-

\\//
ʒſ Joe Asks...
~   __What If I Don't Have Anyone to Talk To?__

If you don't have someone to play the role of cardboard cutout, all is not necessarily lost. Try scribbling down a narrative of the problem on paper or perhaps composing an email to a friend. The trick is not to censor yourself—just like a writer would.

times, the person who's helping you doesn't even have to say a word—they might just as well be a cardboard cutout[6] (or rubber duck, wooden Indian, or any of the other myriad inanimate objects this effect has been named after).

There are excellent reasons why things work this way—explaining your problem to someone else forces you to get your thoughts in order, enumerate your assumptions, and construct an argument from basic principles. Very often, putting that structure in place is all it takes for you to see the solution yourself. And if not, what have you lost?

> Explaining the problem helps get your thoughts in order.

Role-Play

Role-playing can be a helpful way to explain and explore problems, especially those involving interactions between largely independent systems. "You play client 1, I'll be client 2, and Fred can play the server—now how do we set up an interclient session?"

Don't forget to use props if appropriate. Index cards can represent messages exchanged over the network. Or whoever is holding the stuffed "Tux" doll owns the database lock. Most development rooms I've been in are full of bits and pieces collected from various trade shows over the years—make them work for you for a change.

---

6.   An ex-colleague of mine kept an actual cardboard cutout of Posh Spice, Victoria Beckham (or Adams as she was at the time), for this purpose. Or at least that's why he told us he had it.

Let Problems Lie Fallow

You spent a frustrating day making no progress against a seemingly intractable problem. In disgust, you call it a day. That evening, while you're doing something completely unconnected to the problem, the answer pops fully formed into your head. While you were cooking supper, talking to your mother on the phone, and reading bedtime stories to the kids, your subconscious was steadily working on the problem. And it has just worked its magic again.

> Help your subconscious help you.

This happens to all of us—the scales fall from our eyes, and what was previously opaque is suddenly perfectly transparent. The bad news is that there's no way to choreograph this effect. Sometimes your subconscious will deliver the goods, and other times it will remain stubbornly silent. But there are certainly things you can do to help.

If you find yourself getting frustrated or *thrashing* (lots of action but little forward progress), that can be a sign that you need to take a break. Work on a different problem for a while, make a cup of tea, take a walk, practice your juggling for a while—anything that will take your mind off the problem.

At worst, you'll return to the problem refreshed and more likely to make significant progress. And at best, if you're lucky, the magic will happen, and your subconscious will deliver the goods.

When the stroke of genius arrives out of nowhere, write it down. If a pen and paper isn't available, send yourself an SMS or tell whoever you happen to be with—there's nothing more frustrating than being unable to recall your insight the following day.

Particularly difficult problems can benefit from a longer break. The fresh perspective of a new morning often helps immeasurably. But beware of overdoing it—tracking down an involved bug means that you need to understand a lot of different things. Take too much time off, and you might find that you're having to remind yourself of too much. And some bugs, unfortunately, are resistant to shortcuts and will submit only to sustained pressure.

Change Something. Anything!

As we've already discussed, it's very important that you think carefully about your experiments. You should know *why* you're running them and *what* you expect them to tell you.

But sometimes, if you're completely stuck, it's worth just making a change for its own sake. Any change. Probably it won't tell you anything, but sometimes it will surprise you—and surprises always teach you something.

Not What I Thought Was Going On at All
by Matthew Rudy Jacobs

I had a bug recently that seemed to be "a form multiselect intermittently doesn't autoselect." It was jumping between being empty and what I expected.

Each time I reproduced the problem, I was using the same inputs ("Fire" and "Health") or leaving the field blank.

After spending a while dumbfounded, I tried a different data set ("Charities" and "Probation"). To my surprise, it still jumped intermittently between "Fire" and "Health" and being empty. The problem had nothing to do with defaulting—it was that the form was cached (on two different servers), and I was missing this fact because I was always using the same select options.

The Sherlock Holmes Principle

Sherlock Holmes famously said, "When you have eliminated the impossible, whatever remains, however improbable, must be the truth."

> When you have eliminated the impossible, whatever remains, however improbable, must be the truth.

It is a valuable reminder that, although most of the time simple explanations are the most likely, sometimes what's going on really is weird. Occasionally, all the planets really do align in just the right way—don't reject an explanation just because it seems too unlikely to be true.

It's Always the Butler
by Frederick Cheung

One of the controllers in my Ruby on Rails application was claiming that its start() action didn't exist. The code hadn't changed in months, and I could see the method definition in the source—so, what was stopping Rails from finding it?

I fired up my trusty debugger and went stepping through ActionController. For security reasons, not all methods should be exposed as actions, so Rails removes anything defined in ActionController::Base. For some reason, ActionController::Base had suddenly gained a method called start()—mystery solved.

Except that I couldn't find where this start() was coming from. It certainly wasn't anywhere in the source. I fired up the interactive console to do some more digging, and the mystery deepened—no start(), even though I was running the same code.

After a lot of to-ing and fro-ing and following blind alleys, it finally occurred to me that the problem was the debugger itself. I had a look at the source of the debugger, and sure enough, it defines Kernel#start(), which was being imported into ActionController. So, the seemingly random factor that was causing the action to fade in and out of existence was whether or not I was debugging something else.

Persevere

Although on occasion it may not seem like it, there is no such thing as a bug that can't be diagnosed. All the software running on any computer is created by humans, and we can always extract enough information to understand precisely what it's doing. In this way, software is very different from almost any other field of human endeavor.

Of course, this doesn't in any way mean that diagnosis is easy. But when you're despairing that you will ever get to the bottom of the current problem, keep in mind that there's always a way through. Given enough time, effort, and determination, you *will* get there.

3.6 Validate Your Diagnosis

We humans are multitalented creatures. Unfortunately, one of our talents is self-deception—we're very good at convincing ourselves of something we want to be true. With that in mind, time spent validating that your diagnosis really stands up to scrutiny is time very well spent.

- Explain your diagnosis to someone else. They might spot a flaw, or the cardboard cutout effect might work its magic allowing you to do so.

- Check out a pristine copy of the source code, without any of the changes you've made along the way, and verify that your analysis still holds. You may have been careful not to introduce any unintended side effects, but nothing gives you more confidence that you succeeded than starting again from a known-good copy.

- Now that you understand the problem, are there any other ways in which you can prove that it really does work the way that you think it does? Try them quickly—do you see what you expect to?

- Play devil's advocate, and imagine that you *are* wrong—what mistake did you make?

These checks and balances shouldn't take long, and I hope they will just convince you that you were right after all. If not, then they have saved you both embarrassment and time, a very worthwhile exercise indeed.

Now that you have a diagnosis you trust, all that remains is implementing the fix, which is what we'll cover in the next chapter.

3.7 Put It in Action

- Construct hypotheses, and test them with experiments.
  - Make sure you understand what your experiments are going to tell you.
  - Make only one change at a time.
  - Keep a record of what you've tried.
  - Ignore nothing.
- When things aren't going well:
  - If the changes you're making don't seem to be having an effect, you're not changing what you think you are.
  - Validate your assumptions.
  - Are you facing multiple interacting causes or a changing underlying system?
- Validate your diagnosis.

Chapter 4

Fix

So, you've completed your diagnosis. It's time to pat yourself on the back—chances are that you've completed the hardest part of your task. Now that you understand the problem, fixing it should be a breeze.

Be careful, however. Up until now, your focus has been on doing whatever it takes to work out just what exactly has been going on and why your software has been misbehaving. You've created ad hoc experiments, modified the code to insert logging, forced error conditions to arise, or otherwise bent the software to your will. You've cultivated a deliberately creative and open frame of mind as you've thought up and subsequently proved or disproved various different hypotheses.

Now you're about to embark on an altogether different kind of exercise. The "anything goes" flavor of diagnosis needs to be replaced with the more disciplined and structured approach required to create high-quality, accurate, and trustworthy modifications to the source. In short, you're no longer a sleuth—it's time to be a software engineer again.

Your primary goal, of course, is to fix the problem. But there's more to a good fix than just making the software behave correctly—you also need to lay the groundwork for the future. Without care, software can quickly fall foul of entropy, or *bit rot* as it's often known.

> There's more to a good fix than just making the software behave correctly.

One fix after another, and, little by little, your originally clean design is lost underneath a patchwork of inadequately thought-out changes.

In this chapter, we'll explore how to simultaneously achieve the following goals:

- Fixing the problem
- Avoiding introducing regressions
- Maintaining or improving the overall quality (readability, architecture, test coverage, performance, and so on) of the code

4.1 Clearing the Decks

Before diving in and starting to design your fix, there's some housekeeping to perform. The first order of business is to ensure that you start from a clean slate.

While hot on the heels of the problem, you've likely modified source files and configuration settings, created experiments on the fly, and left data files lying around. You don't want to end up accidentally checking in any of these ad hoc changes. If you don't clean up before starting to make the changes you *do* want to check in, there's a danger that you'll find it hard to tell one from the other.

You don't want to simply discard everything, however, because there's a good chance that some of the changes you've made, or data files you created during diagnosis, will form an excellent basis for the test cases you're about to write as part of the fix. Here, as in so many other situations, your source control system proves its value.

First, you need to perform a quick audit of the changes you've made.[1] Don't skip this step. You'll be amazed how often you discover changes you'd forgotten about.

> **Start from a clean source tree.**

Often, discarding these changes will be the right thing to do.[2] If, however, there are changes you want to hold on to, resist the temptation to leave them in place and modify the code around them. Remember that one of our goals is to avoid regressions, and these changes haven't been made in such a way that means they can be trusted. Feel free to take notes, or a copy of relevant files, but when you start implementing a fix, it's crucial to start from a

---

1. svn status followed by svn diff if you're using Subversion.
2. svn revert --recursive

clean source tree. If the changes you made during diagnosis were particularly far reaching, it may even be easier to check out a whole fresh source tree and start from there, leaving the polluted tree around as a reference.

This gives you a trustworthy starting point. The next thing to think about is how you're going to prove to yourself that your fix really does address the problem at hand.

4.2 Testing

Let's assume that your development process includes test-first (or test-driven) development and that you have, therefore, an automated test framework and an extensive body of unit tests in place already. It's now, when you're about to start making changes to the source, that this approach really pays off. Not only can you use it to ensure that your fix addresses the problem, but it also provides an invaluable safeguard against regressions.

Because you're going to rely on the tests so heavily, start by ensuring that they all pass (which should certainly be the case because you've just ensured that you're working on a

> Start by ensuring that all your tests pass.

clean source tree). If they don't all pass, stop immediately, and determine why. Maybe a colleague checked in a broken change? Or something in your local environment is configured incorrectly? Whatever, if the tests don't pass, you can't use them to help with the changes you're about to make.

One of the rules of test-first development is that you shouldn't modify the source until you have a failing test. So, having demonstrated that you're standing on the firm foundation of a test suite that passes all the tests, you had better make sure you have one that fails.

Given that a bug slipped through, clearly either your existing tests don't adequately test the functionality in question or the tests are themselves broken. Consequently, you either need to add one or more new tests or fix the existing ones.

Here's the sequence to follow:

1. Run the existing tests, and demonstrate that they pass.
2. Add one or more new tests, or fix the existing tests, to demonstrate the bug (in other words, to fail).

3. Fix the bug.

4. Demonstrate that your fix works (the failing tests no longer fail).

5. Demonstrate that you haven't introduced any regressions (none of the tests that previously passed now fail).

Of course, in reality (and depending upon just how intricate a fix you're dealing with), the process is unlikely to be as neatly linear as this. You're likely to have to iterate between constructing tests and modifying code several times as you work toward the final solution.

The experiments, data files, and anything else you created to reproduce and diagnose the problem form a rich source of ideas. With luck, in fact, all you need to do is tidy up and formalize what you created then. Remember, however, that what we're trying to do here is come up with something of production quality. Tests created while you didn't really understand the problem may well be a good starting point, but you should take the time to ensure that they're well constructed and test everything that needs to be tested.

> Make sure you know how you're going to test it before designing your fix.

What if you're not using test-first development? Even then, testing remains critical. If you don't have a reliable test that demonstrates the problem, how can you be sure that you've fixed it? The major difference is that the test may be something you perform manually rather than automatically and that you discard after you're done. Oh, and you're going to have to be really careful because in the absence of a set of regression tests, the chances of accidentally introducing a regression are much higher.

How My Test Suite Saved My Ass
by Dominic Binks

I was working on an application written in PHP. Luckily, we had an extensive suite of automated tests. I made a change (a really simple one), and the tests broke on a web service interface that I hadn't touched. Certainly my change had nothing to do with it.

Sigh.

It turns out the reason the test failed was that the web service was returning invalid XML. I looked at the XML, and it looked valid to me. I'm no XML guru, so I got a colleague to look at it, and he said it looked valid too. I had always been led to believe that XML was relatively simple—certainly it should be easy to see whether it's well formed.

Eventually I tracked down a stray newline at the start of the XML document, which is illegal in XML—hence the XML document was reported as invalid.

So, how was that stray newline appearing? Well, I had accidentally added a newline to the end of the file after the closing <*php*> tag. The result is that the PHP processor interpreted it as a piece of HTML to be sent to the "browser."

Normally an extra newline would make no different whatsoever. However, when the PHP code was added into the web service code path, the newline got emitted before the rest of the XML document, which led to the invalid XML.

Without the autotests, this would have probably gone into production and then would need to be pulled to figure out why part of the service wasn't working anymore.

4.3 Fix the Cause, Not the Symptoms

Some years ago, when working on embedded code written in C, I tracked a bug down to a function that looked something like this:

```
int process_items(item* item_array, int array_size)
{
    int i;

    /* For some reason array_size is off by one, so fix it up here */
    array_size++;

    for(i = 0; i < array_size; i++) {
        «Process item_array[i]»
    }
}
```

The developer in question (whose blushes I will save) had correctly determined, some months earlier, that the bug he was working on was "caused" by a bad value for array_size. However, instead of continuing his analysis to determine why the function was being called with a bad argument, he decided to make the bug "go away" by fixing it up in the function.

Of course, as I subsequently discovered, it turned out that process_items() could be called from multiple locations, and, very occasionally, array_size wasn't off by one. This resulted in an array overflow that (this being C) caused obscure problems that only surfaced later and required quite a bit of effort to track down.

\/⁄ Joe Asks...
ᴗᶠ
Is It Ever OK to "Paper Over the Cracks?"

Sometimes, even if we do understand the root cause, there's still a temptation to "paper over the cracks." Perhaps the bug is deeply rooted in the architecture, and a true fix would involve dangerously widespread changes. Or there might be a danger of introducing compatibility issues with previous versions (see Section 8.2, *Backward Compatibility*, on page 118). Or a true fix might simply be much more effort than a judiciously applied patch.

Well, this is a pragmatic book, and as such, it would be foolish for us to deny that there are occasions where this isn't the right approach. They are, however, *very* rare.

Every occasion where we choose not to address the root cause of a problem, we are significantly reducing the overall quality of the codebase. This doesn't just have practical implications but also psychological (see Section 7.1, *No Broken Windows*, on page 105).

So yes, there are occasions where it is appropriate for us to choose not to address the underlying problem—but only as a means of last resort and only with our eyes open to the consequences.

Unfortunately, this kind of thing occurs all too frequently. All of us will, at some time in our careers, find ourselves chasing such a bug.

There are two reasons why we end up making this kind of mistake. Most frequently it is because we haven't taken our analysis far enough and haven't yet uncovered the true root cause of the problem. Occasionally it can arise as a misguided response to time pressure.

Let's take the last of these, time pressure, first. Somewhere in the world, there may be a software engineering project that doesn't operate under constant time pressure. I've never worked on such a project, though. Even if you're lucky enough to find yourself in this happy situation, the users affected by the bug you're working on are unlikely to want to wait a minute more than they have to for the fix.

The upshot is that you're very likely to be under pressure to just "make the bug go away" and move onto the next task. In the cold light of day, it's easy to vow never to do such a thing, but in the heat of the moment, with irate users shouting at you on one side and impatient managers on the other, the temptation can be almost irresistible.

However bad giving in to this temptation might be, it's nothing compared to the dangers associated with fixing a bug before you fully understand the root cause. At least if you understand the root cause and take an educated (if misguided) decision to implement a quick workaround, you understand the implications of your actions. If you don't really understand what's going on, it's effectively impossible to predict the effect that your actions will have.

Recall that fixing the problem at hand is only one of three goals we've set ourselves. We also need to avoid introducing regressions and maintain the overall quality of the code. Our focus naturally tends to be on the first goal, but the second two are just as important (from a long-term point of view, possibly even more important). With this in mind, making changes we don't understand is therefore the height of recklessness.

How do you know when you really understand the root cause of a problem? Well, there are some rules of thumb (for example, would I feel comfortable explaining this to a colleague, and would my explanation entail the use of phrases like "For some reason. . . " or "I'm not sure why, but. . . "). But the simple truth of the matter is that most of the time you *know* whether you understand the root cause. What is called for here is intellectual honesty—the courage to admit to yourself that, even though you seem to have found a way to fix the bug, you haven't yet reached the point where you can be confident that you really understand the cause, and you can't, therefore, trust your fix.

4.4 Refactoring

The last few years have seen a sea change in software development with the increasing popularity of agile approaches. As far as code construction (as opposed to project management) is concerned, the most significant effect has been the widespread adoption of two techniques—automated testing and refactoring.

Refactoring is the process of improving the design of existing code *without changing its behavior*. It is this latter, and sometimes overlooked, aspect of refactoring that will mostly concern us here. For a

Joe Asks...

What Are the Key Insights of Refactoring?

Many people's reaction to refactoring when first exposed to it is "so what?" This is just "tidying up" the code, something that programmers have been doing for almost as long as programmers have existed. Certainly, to some extent all that Martin Fowler did when he published *Refactoring* was to catalog techniques that developers have been using for years.

But there's more to refactoring than just a catalog of useful techniques. It relies on Fowler's two key insights:

- Modifying existing code can be carried out safely only with the safety net of a comprehensive suite of unit tests.

- We should never attempt to refactor the code at the same time as modifying its behavior.

In other words, you can modify the behavior of the code, or you can refactor it. You should never attempt to do both at the same time.

Upon reflection, it's easy to see why this is the case. Imagine that you attempt to modify both the structure of your code and its functionality at the same time, and after doing so one of your tests fails. This might indicate that you made a mistake when modifying its structure. Or it might be an expected result of the change in functionality. It's difficult, however, to be sure which. The more complicated the change in functionality or structure, the harder it is to be certain.

By doing only one or the other, you avoid this issue entirely and can forge ahead with potentially far-reaching refactorings involving dramatic changes to the code with confidence.

full introduction to refactoring, see Martin Fowler's classic *Refactoring* [FBB+99].

Bug fixing often uncovers opportunities for refactoring. The very fact that you're working with code that contains a bug indicates that there is a chance that it could be clearer or better structured. It is very likely that you will spot areas of code that could be improved as you go.

Furthermore, the changes necessary to fix the bug may well, if performed naïvely, introduce duplication that should be DRYed up (according to the Don't Repeat Yourself principle described in *The Pragmatic Programmer* [HT00]).

Performing these refactorings is every bit as important as fixing the bug (remember that one of our goals is to maintain or improve the overall quality of the code). There will be occasions where you choose to refactor after fixing and other occasions where it makes sense to refactor first (because doing so gets you to a state where it's easier to fix the bug). Occasionally, when working on a particularly intricate fix, you'll iterate back and forth between refactoring and bug fixing.

But remember that refactoring should never be combined with modifying the functionality of the code, and that very definitely includes fixing bugs.

> Refactor or change functionality—one or the other, never both.

This leads us on to the topic of interacting with source control when fixing bugs.

4.5 Checking In

Our source control system is one of the most powerful weapons in our armory. We can squander much of its value if we don't use it carefully, though.

It can be tempting to collect a number of small changes together and—in one go—check them all in. You're on a roll, after all, and it would be a pity to break the flow. Unfortunately, doing so significantly decreases the utility of using source control.

From the point of view of debugging, source control's main value is as an audit trail. If someone does introduce a regression, you should be able to find out exactly which change did so (and therefore what you need to do to fix it) by searching back through previous versions (see Section 3.2, *Leveraging Source Control*, on page 50). The effectiveness of this approach is inversely proportional to the size of each check-in, however. Discovering which check-in introduced a bug is of little value if the check-in in question includes changes to hundreds of files scattered throughout the project.

One logical change,
one check-in.

To avoid this problem, stick to the rule *one logical change, one check-in*.

For simple fixes, this may mean a single check-in, but most cases involve more than one logical change (and therefore more than one check-in). If the fix requires two logically independent changes to the functionality and two independent refactorings, that probably means four independent check-ins.

As ever, you should use your judgment. It's probably overkill to use three check-ins for a fix requiring three single-line changes, even if each is independent of the others. But if you err on the side of checking in early and often, you will rarely go wrong. And remember that you can also help a great deal by ensuring that your check-in comments are as meaningful (and specific) as possible.

Diff before check-in.

One final point—whether fixing bugs or implementing new functionality, it's good practice to always examine exactly what it is that you're about to check in before every check-in.[3] It won't take long, and every once in a while, you'll catch a change that you really didn't intend to make from slipping through.

4.6 Get Your Code Reviewed

No matter how careful you are, sooner or later you're going to create an intended fix that makes things worse rather than better. This is particularly true when it comes to code quality and maintainability, which no amount of testing (automated or otherwise) is able to guarantee. Code reviews, formal or otherwise, are an extremely good means to catch problems like this before they do any permanent damage.

Reviews are an intrinsic part of some development methodologies. XP, for example, ensures that two pairs of eyes see every change via pair programming. It doesn't have to be a formal element of your methodology to be useful, however.

Who and When?

There is no single right time for a review. On occasion, getting a colleague involved in the very early stages of a fix is appropriate. On

---

3. svn diff if you're using Subversion.

other occasions, you might ask them to simply sign off on a completed change.

The rule of thumb is to consider a review whenever you reach an area of uncertainty or risk. Remember that reviews aren't one-time-only things—there's no rule that you can't ask for help repeatedly if it makes sense to do so.

As for who to ask to perform the review, you're likely to reap significant benefit whoever does so. Simply having a second pair of eyes examine your work is a big step forward. If you're working in an area that's relatively new to you, it probably makes sense to ask someone who is already familiar with it (the original author, for example). By contrast, if you know the code extremely well, consider asking someone who is new to it and has a fresh perspective.

Successfully fixing the bug is a great milestone, but it's not the end of the process. Before moving on to the next task, take a moment to reflect upon how the problem snuck into your software in the first place. Are there any other instances of the same issue elsewhere, and could it happen again?

4.7 Put It in Action

- Bug fixing involves three goals:
    - Fix the problem.
    - Avoid introducing regressions.
    - Maintain or improve overall quality (readability, architecture, test coverage, and so on) of the code.
- Start from a clean source tree.
- Ensure that the tests pass before making any changes.
- Work out how you're going to test your fix before making changes.
- Fix the cause, not the symptoms.
- Refactor, but never at the same time as modifying functionality.
- One logical change, one check-in.

Chapter 5

Reflect

Bug fixing, by its very nature, tends to be tightly focused. You're working on a very specific problem, and the chances are that, more often than not, the fix will involve an isolated area of code. Despite this narrow focus, you need to keep your eye on the big picture. To that end, it's well worth taking a few moments of reflection after implementing your fix.

In this chapter, we'll consider the following:

- How did it ever work?
- When and why did the problem slip through the cracks?
- Ensuring that the problem never happens again.

5.1 How Did It Ever Work?

One of the humorous emails that turns up in my inbox every once in a while is entitled "The six stages of debugging" and reads as follows:

1. That can't happen.
2. That doesn't happen on my machine.
3. That shouldn't happen.
4. Why is that happening?
5. Oh, I see.
6. How did that ever work?

As with most humor, it's funny because it's based in truth. In particular, it's not at all unusual to find yourself thinking "How did that ever work?" after you've completed your diagnosis.

If you do find yourself thinking this, pause for a moment. It's a good sign that you haven't really fully understood all the possible implications of the bug. Keep going until you understand how it *did* ever work—there's an excellent chance that you will learn something in the process.

Not As Secure As We Thought

We had a suite of web applications that delegated security to a shared "gatekeeper" application, enabling a single username and password to work for all. If the user had logged into any application in the suite, they could use any other without logging in again, all controlled through an encrypted cookie stored in the user's browser.

I found myself working on a bug in which one particular user was unable to log in—it turned out that under certain circumstances, the code that generated the cookie could go wrong. It was easily fixed once I'd worked out what was wrong, so it was another bug squashed.

But I had a nagging doubt. The circumstances in which the cookie was generated incorrectly weren't *that* obscure. Why was only one user having problems? How was everyone else able to log in successfully? Something was up.

Sure enough, deeper investigation demonstrated that the system wasn't as secure as we had intended it to be. It was supposed to be changing the secret used to encrypt the cookie periodically, but this turned out to be broken. So, users who would otherwise have fallen foul of the bug I'd just fixed weren't doing so, because they were able to continue to use an old cookie.

If I hadn't listened to the little voice in the back of my mind saying "Something is wrong—you don't really understand what's going on yet," we would never have found this.

Kent Beck talks about a similar effect in *Test-Driven Development* [Bec02]. Occasionally, we find that we write a test expecting it to fail, but in fact it passes. When this happens, invariably it teaches us something important.

But there's something missing from these six steps. There should really be a seventh—"It'll never happen again!" In the next sections, we'll look at what you can do to ensure that it doesn't.

5.2   What Went Wrong?

The first step toward learning the lessons of the bug is determining what went wrong.

The Five Whys

A useful trick when performing root cause analysis is to ask "Why?" five times. For example:

- The software crashed. Why?
- The code didn't handle network failure during data transmission. Why?
- There was no unit test to check for network failure. Why?
- The original developer wasn't aware that he should create such a test. Why?
- None of our unit tests check for network failure. Why?
- We failed to take network failure into account in the original design.

Why five? It's just a rule of thumb—sometimes you will need fewer steps, sometimes more. And sometimes it won't help at all (it will help you identify only the root causes you already know about). But it can be helpful, and five seems to be about right in most cases.

Haven't We Just Done That?

Isn't determining what went wrong exactly what diagnosis is all about? Yes it is, but what we're talking about here is the bigger picture—how did the mistake make its way into the software in the first place?

For example, your diagnosis might be that the bug was caused by a failure to take into account the possibility of a network outage while receiving data from a server. That's as far as you need to go during diagnosis. What we're looking to do here is to work out why the original developer of the code didn't realize that they had to handle network failure.

Root Cause Analysis

The fact that a bug crept into the code in the first place means that something went wrong somewhere in your process. When, exactly? And why?

Requirements:

   Were the requirements complete and correct? Perhaps they were ambiguous, interpreted incorrectly, or misunderstood?

Blame

Proactively identifying process issues can work wonders for overall quality. Be careful, however—the object is to learn lessons, not to apportion blame.

Yes, someone somewhere probably screwed up, but we all make mistakes occasionally. Pointing the finger is unlikely to be productive or helpful.

A blame culture is corrosive, eroding the team ethos that is vital for success. If they fear that they will be pilloried or punished for their mistakes, your colleagues will start worrying more about how to protect their back than doing what's best for the team and wider organization. In the worst cases, this can even lead to lying, setting up fall guys, and other dysfunctional behavior.

Leading by example is particularly powerful, for good or for ill. If you start ranting about the culprit after tracking down a particularly sticky problem, other members of the team are likely to adopt the same behavior. If, by contrast, a problem of your own making comes to light, own up and admit mea culpa to demonstrate that there's nothing to be ashamed about. How you handle a problem after it comes to light is more important than the fact that the problem existed in the first place.

Architecture or design:
> Was there an oversight within the architecture or design—something we failed to take into account or allow for? Or perhaps they're fine, but we failed to follow the design correctly?

Testing:
> Did we have adequate tests covering this area? Or maybe the error was in the tests themselves?

Construction:
> This is what most commonly comes to mind when thinking about a bug. Perhaps the author made a simple mistake when writing the code, or maybe they misunderstood some aspect of the underlying technology (libraries, compilers, and so forth).

5.3 It'll Never Happen Again

Once you've identified the source of the error, you can take steps to ensure that it doesn't happen again. In some cases, this might mean nothing more than a "note to self" to be more careful in that area in the future, or a quiet word with a colleague to let them know about their mistake. On other occasions, it might be something to raise at your next end-of-iteration post-mortem—especially if you've noticed a pattern of mistakes occurring at a particular point or for a particular reason. Very occasionally, it may be time to "ring the alarm bells."

Automatic Validation

Something to keep a watchful eye for are problem areas, common mistakes, and other instances of the same problem. Imagine that you've just fixed a memory leak in some C++ code that started out like this:

```
void f(void)
{
    T* pt = new T;

    «Do something with pt»

    delete pt;
}
```

This code is fine, unless one of the functions it calls might throw an exception, in which case pt will not be deleted. There are various ways to fix this, such as by using auto_ptr() from the standard library:

```
void f(void)
{
    auto_ptr<T> pt(new T);

    «Do something with pt»

    // auto_ptr ensures that pt is deleted even if an exception is thrown
}
```

Great—another bug bites the dust. But before moving onto the next, consider whether the original mistake was a one-off. It seems at least possible that the author of the original code might not understand how to write exception-safe code in C++. In which case, might there be other instances of the same issue elsewhere? Rather than wait for the bugs that are possibly lurking undetected to be reported, now is the time to do an audit to see whether there are other examples of the problem and fix them.

Talking to Colleagues

Letting a colleague know that they've made a mistake can be a minefield. On the one hand, it's extremely valuable information—you owe it to them to let them know so that they can avoid the same mistake in the future. On the other hand, we programmers are not always known for our interpersonal skills, and telling someone that they've screwed up can easily go wrong if done without tact.

There are no hard and fast rules. Sometimes, no matter how careful you are, your well-intentioned feedback might be taken badly. But there are certainly things you can do to improve the chances of it being taken in the intended spirit:

- Most important, give feedback for the right reason. If you're *really* telling someone about their mistake because you like the feeling of superiority it gives you, hold your tongue. However you word your "helpful" feedback, your true motivation will be obvious.

- Think before you speak and plan what you're going to say before the conversation. Imagine how you might react if someone said the same thing to you, while bearing in mind that not everyone is the paragon of reason you are. ;-)

- Avoid personal comments. It can be helpful to use "I" and "we" language instead of "you" language.

- Be constructive.

- Remember that you might be mistaken. Don't simply announce that they've made a mistake—explore the possibility with them. You may discover that they had good reason for their actions, that the fault wasn't theirs, or that you've misdiagnosed the problem.

Even better, can you find a way to automatically detect errors of this type so that we avoid similar problems in the future? In Section 10.3, *Resource Leaks and Exception Handling*, on page 172, we will discuss a technique that allows exactly this kind of problem to be automatically detected. And it turns out that we can achieve the same for a wide variety of errors.

Most projects of any size tend to accrete their own foibles over time. *Before you create a new customer, make sure that you update the accounts table first*—that kind of thing. Wherever these kind of rules exist, it's possible for someone to get them wrong, and often there's no way to avoid doing so unless you just happen to know the pitfalls. In Chapter 10, *Teach Your Software to Debug Itself*, on page 157, we will discuss how you can create self-debugging software that automatically alerts you if you inadvertently fall foul of this kind of thing.

Refactor

Something else to consider is whether the code is leading people astray. If you notice several examples of a particular problem, maybe the structure or the interface is making it too easy to make the same mistake repeatedly?

Imagine that you notice that people tend to pass the wrong arguments to the following C function:

```
void drawRectangle(int x, int y, int width, int height,
    bool border, bool fill, bool client_coordinates);
```

If you think about what a typical call might look like, it becomes obvious why people struggle to get the arguments right. For example:

```
drawRectangle(10, 10, 30, 50, true, true, false);
```

This could hardly be described as self-documenting. Changing the definition to something along the following lines, however:

```
const int NO_BORDER = 0x00;
const int DRAW_BORDER = 0x01;
const int NO_FILL = 0x00;
const int FILL_BODY = 0x02;
const int GLOBAL_COORDINATES = 0x00;
const int CLIENT_COORDINATES = 0x04;

void drawRectangle(int x, int y, int width, int height,
    unsigned int options);
```

means that it can now be called like this:

```
drawRectangle(10, 10, 30, 50,
    DRAW_BORDER | FILL_BODY | GLOBAL_COORDINATES);
```

That is much clearer (and much harder to get wrong).[1]

Process

The benefit of the techniques we've just looked at is that they're unequivocal. An improved interface that makes incorrect use impossible completely removes the opportunity to make the same mistake again. An automatic check will always detect the issue it's looking for. So, if you can address the root cause this way, you should.

Unfortunately, it's not always possible to find a way to completely eliminate the opportunity to make a mistake, and examining your process might be your only remaining option.

Perhaps you need to look at the quality of your requirements documentation? Or consider introducing design reviews? Maybe a checklist of common pitfalls to watch for during code reviews would prove useful?

5.4 Close the Loop

The project that you are working on will have its own set of norms, for example:

- Coding standards
- Testing standards
- Documentation standards
- Reporting/tracking processes
- Design guidelines
- Performance requirements

Whenever you fix a bug, you need to bear these in mind. Do you need to update the end-user documentation as a result of the fix? Or the change log for the next release? Does the work need to be tracked against a particular client or project? Do you need to resolve a ticket in your

---

1. If you're lucky enough to be working in a language that supports named arguments, you won't need to jump through these hoops.

bug-tracking package? Or hand it off to the QA department (and what supporting materials do they need)?

So, that's it—we've covered the life cycle of a bug all the way from reproduction through diagnosis, fixing and reflection. In the next section, we'll look at the bigger picture—how do we find out that there's a problem to be addressed in the first place, and how does bug fixing fit into the software life cycle?

5.5 Put It in Action

- Take the time to perform a root cause analysis:
    - At what point in your process did the error arise?
    - What went wrong?
- Ensure that the same problem can't happen again:
    - Automatically check for problems.
    - Refactor code to remove the opportunity for incorrect usage.
    - Talk to your colleagues, and modify your process if appropriate.
- Close the loop with other stakeholders.

Part II

The Bigger Picture

Chapter 6

Discovering That
You Have a Problem

In the first part of the book, we started from the point at which we already knew that we had a bug. In this chapter, we'll look at what comes before this.

Bugs can come to light at any point in the software development cycle— from seconds after the code is written to months or years after it's released. Ideally, you'll find them yourself and as early as possible— it's easier to fix bugs that are detected quickly, and doing so avoids the embarrassment (or worse) of allowing a bug to escape into the wild.

Nevertheless, there will be occasions where, despite your best efforts, a customer is affected by a bug. In this chapter, we'll talk about what happens after they have been. Specifically, we'll cover the following:

- Tracking bugs

- Working with users

- Working with the customer support and QA teams

6.1 Tracking Bugs

Whatever kind of software you're working on, you're going to need to create some process through which your users can tell you about problems (and ultimately, through which you can tell them about fixes).

Bug-Tracking Systems

Bug-tracking systems vary dramatically in size, scope, and approach. At one end of the scale are simple single-purpose systems, and at the other end are fully fledged workflow management systems that control and log every aspect of the software development process (of which bug tracking is just one small part). Nevertheless, the basic goals of a bug-tracking system remain constant:

- First and foremost, it ensures that we don't forget about a bug.
- By providing a standard format for bug reports, it increases the chance that all relevant information will be included.
- As an audit trail, it ensures that for each release we know which bugs are outstanding, which were fixed, by whom and how. It can be an important source of information for release notes (we might even be able to automatically generate them).
- It allows us to prioritize bugs and determine which to work on first.
- By providing a means of communication between various stakeholders, it ensures that everyone understands the current state of the bug and that all relevant information is provided as responsibility moves between individuals or teams.
- As a management tool, it provides an overview of the current state of the project.
- On the rare occasion we choose *not* to fix a bug, we can store the reasoning behind that decision so we don't have to repeat the process in the future.

However good your bug-tracking system, it's only as good as the information it contains.

What Makes a Good Bug Report?

We've all experienced the frustration of having to deal with an unhelpful bug report, something that says little more than "it's broken" and gives you nothing more to go on. So, we know what we *don't* want, but in an ideal world what would we see in a bug report?

At first glance, it's obvious—whatever information is necessary to allow us to diagnose the problem. Unfortunately, until we've performed that diagnosis, we don't know what might and what might not be relevant. So, a good bug report errs on the side of more rather than less.

> \//
> ꙷꙷ **Joe Asks...**
> ꙷ
>
> **Do I Need to Track My Bugs Electronically?**
>
> Because we work with it every day, there is a natural tendency for us to assume that all problems should be solved with technology. On occasion, however, it can just get in the way.
>
> If you're working in a small colocated team, don't have many bugs to track, and don't need to provide remote access to your bug database, then a nontechnical solution (index cards stuck to a whiteboard?) may well be right for you.
>
> Don't confuse a low-technology system with a casual approach, though. Handling bugs responsibly is a key part of professional software development—just because your bug reports are handwritten doesn't mean that you can treat them any less carefully.

It should be *specific, unambiguous,* and *detailed.* If an error message was displayed, what exactly did it say? If data became corrupted, how? Precisely what actions led up to the problem? If the output was incorrect, in what way? If there are supporting resources (input files that reproduce the problem, screenshots of incorrect output, and so forth), these should be attached to the report.

> A report should be specific, unambiguous, and detailed...

As a counterpoint to the previous, a bug report should also be *minimal.* If it can be reproduced with a 10,000-line input file, can that file be cut down at all? Which elements of the sequence of actions leading up to the bug are essential, and which can be discarded? If it manifests on one version of the software, are there other versions that don't display the problem?

> ...but also minimal and unique.

Related to this, a bug report should also be *unique.* If the problem has already been reported, reporting it again is unlikely to be helpful (although there may be additional information to add to the existing report).

My Favorite Bug Report

The product I was working on had a catchall exception handler that displayed a "crash screen" in the event that things broke irretrievably. It didn't happen often, thank goodness, but could help considerably when tracking down the cause.

And then we received a bug report that read "The crash screen has no undo button."

You have to hand it to the user who reported it—it would undeniably have been a great feature if we could have implemented it!

Environment and Configuration Reporting

Almost every bug-tracking system has an environment field. If you're working on desktop software, this might be used to record the operating system the bug manifests in. Or for web software the browser.

So far, so good. But is it enough?

There are two reasons why it isn't. The first is that most nontechnical users typically have no idea about their environment. Does your mother know which browser she uses? Do your colleagues in the sales department know which Windows Service Pack they have installed?

Second, and more to the point, computing environments are becoming more complicated and more interconnected all of the time. Is it enough to know that your user is using Firefox to view your site? Almost certainly not—you probably also need to know which exact version of Firefox they're using, what platform they're using it on, which plug-ins they have installed, whether they have cookies and JavaScript enabled, and so on.

> Collect environment and configuration information automatically.

You can cut through this Gordian knot by adding an option to your software to record whichever aspects of the environment might affect its behavior. Sure, for many bugs, much or all of this information will be irrelevant, but if automated, it's virtually free to collect, and you can rely on its accuracy. And when it *is* relevant, it's invaluable.

What Did You Say It Was Again?

For my sins (and it has felt like purgatory on occasion), I've spent much of my career working on software for mobile phones. If you think that users have trouble working out what they're running on their laptop, you should try asking them about their mobile.

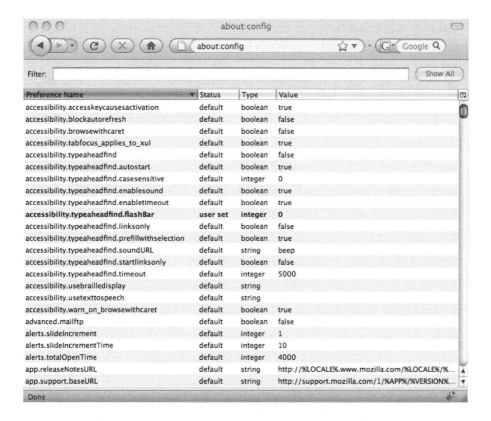

Figure 6.1: FIREFOX'S ABOUT:CONFIG PAGE

Pop quiz (don't look). What make and exact model is your mobile? Not sure? Now take a look. Chances are you're still none the wiser. How exactly are you supposed to work out what it is if you don't already know?

Now imagine what working in technical support must be like when customers can't even answer the most basic questions about their hardware. "Err—it's silver with black buttons. Does that help?"

The same argument applies to any configuration options your software supports. If you provide a means by which this can be recorded automatically, then questions like "Are you *sure* you had feature X enabled?" become a thing of the past.

A good example of this kind of reporting are the various about: URLs supported by many web browsers. Try typing about:config (Figure 6.1), about:buildconfig, or about:cache into Firefox to see what I mean.

6.2 Working with Users

As a software engineer, you understand the value of a bug report. If nobody takes the time and trouble to tell you about problems, you won't find out about them. And you can't fix bugs you don't know about.

Streamline the Process

Unfortunately, there's nothing you can do to guarantee that users will take the time to report bugs or that those they report are of a high quality. But you can increase the likelihood by removing as many barriers as you can.

Make it obvious how to report a bug:
> Place instructions (or better yet, a direct link) to how to report a bug in your software's About dialog box, online help, website, and anywhere else you think appropriate.

Automate:
> Install a top-level exception handler, and give the user the option to file a bug report that automatically contains all the relevant details.

Provide multiple options:
> Some will prefer to report bugs electronically; others will prefer to talk to a human being. Some will prefer email, others an online form.

Keep it simple:
> Each action you ask your users to perform will reduce the number who complete a transaction by half. In other words, ask them to click three times, and only 12.5 percent of them will complete. Five times, and you've reduced that figure to a little more than 3 percent.

Don't have too rigid a template:
> It can be a good idea to have a standard template for bug reports, but beware of making that template too strict. Make sure that you have sensible options for each field including "none of the above."

Respect your users' privacy:
> Your users' data belongs to them, not to you. Make it clear that you understand this with a transparent privacy policy.

Joe Asks...

Surely I Can Rely on My Users to Tell Me About Bugs?

You would think so, wouldn't you? After all, presumably they're using the software because they want to achieve something, and the bug is stopping them from doing so.

Well, whatever you might think, most users won't tell you when things go wrong. Some will assume that it was their fault—that they "clicked the wrong button." Some will sigh resignedly (muttering imprecations under their breath), restart the software, and carry on from where they left off. Others will go to extraordinary lengths to find workarounds for bugs you could fix in seconds.

As a rule of thumb, for every user who tells you about a problem, there will be between 10 and 100 other users who experienced the same problem and didn't think to get in touch.

Effective Communication

Talking to customers can be tricky. Effective communication relies upon shared context, but your point of view is necessarily different from your users'. They don't share your deep understanding of the code, and you don't share their deep understanding of their problem domain. You use different vocabularies, possess different skills, and utilize different problem-solving approaches. You need to be aware of these differences and the issues that potentially arise from them.

There are no simple solutions to these communication issues. All you can do is appreciate that they're inevitable, remain calm, and work your way through them.

Mental Models

We deal with the world by creating mental models. As software engineers, we're particularly aware of this—software is a reification of those models.

Your users create their own mental models too. It may surprise you to discover just how different theirs are from yours, though.

The danger arises when you think that you're both working from the same model. This can lead to myriad misunderstandings that will take a great deal of effort to unpick.

> Imagine how things might appear from your user's perspective.

The most powerful remedy to this situation is to put yourself in the user's shoes and imagine how things might appear from their perspective. Your aim is to tease apart their *observations* (which you can trust) from their *interpretations* (which will be colored by their mental model).

I See What the Problem Is
by Marcus Gröber

I write software for the blind, using speech synthesis on mobile phones, and sometimes I get reports from our users saying "My phone hangs when I do X." But I've learned that what this often really means is "Audio output stops when I do X." The phone becomes so useless without speech that for a blind user it is indistinguishable from a "hang."

Talking to the Nontechnical

Unless you're in the rare situation of creating software that is used by other programmers (in which case you have a slightly different, but no less challenging, set of communication issues), your users probably aren't technically minded. They are unlikely to understand things you take for granted or to appreciate the subtleties involved in diagnosing a problem.

The biggest issue is often extracting accurate details. You know that the slightest detail might be the vital clue, but your user probably doesn't realize how crucial this is. There's an excellent chance that they will paraphrase error messages instead of quoting them exactly or gloss over "irrelevant" details. And they may not react well when you dig deeper to unearth those details.

The only solution is to be patient—explain why the details matter, and talk them through the steps required to collect the relevant data. This can be frustrating—something you could achieve in seconds could well take them much longer—but it's worth the investment of your time.

How Technical Is the Person You're Talking To?
by Vandy Massey

Judging just how technically proficient someone is can be particularly challenging over email or telephone. It's an issue we have to deal with when we're talking to users. Telling them to start Internet Explorer by

---

Users Have No Monopoly on Misunderstanding

You don't get to be a successful software engineer without being bright. Most of us excelled at school and are proud of our intellect. But that doesn't mean that we can't get things wrong.

When it's obvious that there's a misunderstanding, remember that it could be you who's got the wrong idea. You may have a better understanding of the software, but you're unlikely to understand the application area better than your users. That's *their* speciality.

---

saying "Look for the big blue E" is just going to annoy them if they're computer literate, but equally it's surprising just how often we do end up having to talk to users in that sort of language.

I remember how angry I was with the company that developed an EPOS system when I reported a problem with one of their reports. There was a figure being reported on their "end-of-day" report that was consistently wrong. They simply told me that they knew what they were doing and that I was incorrect. They were absolutely set on the idea that because I was a user and therefore "nontechnical," I couldn't possibly know what I was talking about. Even when I told them that I was an accountant by training (and therefore knew perfectly well that the figure on the end-of-day financial report was wrong) and that I had a modest knowledge of development, they dismissed everything I was saying. The problem has never been resolved, so we just work around it because we can. However, I was left with a lasting impression of arrogance, stupidity, and a complete lack of customer focus. I've never bothered to contact them again with any queries, let alone suggestions for upgrades. And we'll definitely not buy any more software from them.

Publish Your Bug Database

Make your bug-tracking system available to all users.[1] If it isn't something you've done before, then allowing everyone to see your "dirty laundry" can be a scary prospect, but the benefits are significant.

---

1. This is extremely easy to achieve if you use a hosted solution—see Section A.1, *Source Control and Issue-Tracking Systems*, on page 193 for some options.

- Seeing that others' reports are taken seriously, responded to, and ultimately addressed gives your users confidence that it's worth their while to take the time to make a report.
- If a user can search your database before reporting a bug, you're much less likely to have duplicate bugs reported.
- One of your users seeing another's bug report may jog a memory or insight that provides the vital clue allowing you to unlock that particular problem.
- Access to existing examples is an excellent way for a user who is unsure to get a feel for what constitutes a helpful bug report.

If you do decide to publish your bug database, remember to make your users aware that information they add to their bug will become public.

Privacy Problems
by Bill Karwin

At one company I worked at, tech support maintained a bug database for years and assumed it was private. When users wanted us to publish this database, we couldn't because it was full of private details about our customers, including names, phone numbers, IP addresses, and so on.

Provide Feedback

When a user submits a bug report, show your gratitude by responding and keeping them in the loop throughout the process.

This need not be an onerous task. Many bug-tracking systems implement the ability to email "interested parties" whenever the status of the bug changes. As long as you keep your bug-tracking system up-to-date, such a system will ensure that whoever reported the bug, plus anyone else you deem appropriate, is kept up-to-date.

Visit the Customer

For really tricky bugs, nothing beats visiting the customer. Watching the user can tell you much more than any bug report.

A Tale of Two Double-Clicks

I was working on what seemed, on the face of things, to be a very simple bug. The bug report described a short sequence of user interface actions and claimed that the bug could be reproduced completely reliably. Try as hard as I might, I couldn't reproduce it and eventually closed it as "works for me."

Within minutes, the program manager who reported it had reopened it and asked me to come over to his desk, where he demonstrated the bug to me several times, completely reliably.

Where it got weird is that whenever I tried to reproduce it—on his computer with him watching and verifying that I was performing the same sequence of actions—it didn't happen.

We eventually worked out that the difference was that when I double-clicked the mouse, I kept it in the same position. He, on the other hand, moved the mouse very slightly between the first and second click. He moved it only a couple of pixels, but this was enough to explain the difference in behavior.

We would never have discovered this without watching each other use the software.

6.3 Working with Support Staff

Most organizations employ a number of technical or semitechnical staff who don't work directly on the construction of the software. Customer support, QA, customer engineering, technical account managers, and so forth, can be an invaluable help during debugging.

Your QA team doesn't only help you by detecting bugs before they make it out into the field. Their expertise and perspective can also be particularly helpful when you're struggling to either find or refine a reproduction. Perhaps you might consider pairing with a colleague from the QA team during this phase of diagnosis?

A good customer support team can really prove their value by bringing their relationship with, and knowledge of, your customers to bear during bug fixing—which can help immeasurably with some of the communication issues we discussed earlier in this chapter. They should be able to use their judgment to ensure that all relevant information is identified and communicated without passing everything along verbatim and overwhelming development with irrelevancies. You might consider asking them to implement a characterization process to improve the quality of bug reports from the field (see the sidebar on the next page).

No matter how good your customer support team is at communicating with users on your behalf, there is a danger that you can become insulated from your users. To foster the intimate understanding of, and empathy with, your users that you need to effectively develop software for them, you might consider working in support occasionally. As well as helping you understand your users,

> Work in customer support occasionally.

Characterization

Sometimes it makes sense for bugs to pass through a *characterization* process before being handed over to the development team for diagnosis. This isn't appropriate in all cases but can be very helpful, particularly for larger projects and teams.

The line between characterization and diagnosis is a fuzzy one, but broadly speaking, it's a *black-box* process, which takes place from "outside" the software without consideration of its internal workings. Diagnosis, by contrast, is a *white-box* process.

The objective of characterization is to find the "boundaries" of the bug. Can it be reproduced reliably? Does it happen on all different platforms or just on one? Can the inputs be varied and still reproduce the problem (and if so, how)?

nothing else will give you a better appreciation of the challenges faced by your colleagues in customer support and respect for their ability.

The Great Wall of QA

Because much of the value your QA team brings to the table is a different perspective, one of the things that they have to guard against is becoming "polluted" with the development team's preconceptions. You can take this too far, however.

I once worked in an organization where there was a *Chinese wall* between development and QA—we weren't allowed to talk to the test team at all. The only information that could flow from development to testing was a compiled binary. The only information that could pass back in the opposite direction was a "pass" or "fail."

When I asked the architect of this team structure why he thought it made sense, he answered that if we were allowed to talk to the test team, we might create software that was constructed in order to pass the tests by "cheating." While this may be theoretically possible, the cure was much worse than the imagined disease.

In the next chapter, we'll turn our attention to psychology—what constitutes an effective debugging mind-set?

6.4 Put It in Action

- Make the most of your bug-tracking system:

    - Pick one at an appropriate level of complexity for your partic-ular situation.

    - Make it directly available to your users.

    - Automate environment and configuration reporting to ensure accurate reports.

- Aim for bug reports that are the following:

    - Specific

    - Unambiguous

    - Detailed

    - Minimal

    - Unique

- When working with users, do the following:

    - Streamline the bug-reporting process as much as possible.

    - Communication is key—be patient and imagine yourself in the user's shoes.

- Foster a good relationship with customer support and QA so you can leverage their support during bug fixing.

Chapter 7

Pragmatic Zero Tolerance

How does bug fixing integrate with the wider software development process? How do you estimate how long it will take to fix a bug or to fix all the bugs currently within your software? How do you ensure that your project doesn't end up struggling in the tar pit of endless bug fixing described so eloquently by Brooks in *The Mythical Man Month* [Bro95]?

In this chapter, we'll cover the following:

- When to fix bugs

- The debugging mind-set

- How to dig yourself out of a quality hole

7.1 Bugs Take Priority

Some teams choose to fix bugs as soon as they come to light (*early* bug fixing). Others "save them up" until the end of the development cycle (*late* bug fixing). Of these, early bug fixing is by far the superior strategy.

Early bug fixing depends upon two principles:

- Processes that are likely to uncover bugs (testing, code reviews, getting running software into users' hands) happen continuously during development.

- Bug fixing takes priority over everything else.

The aim is to keep the number of bugs in the software (both those we know about and those we haven't yet found) as small as possible.

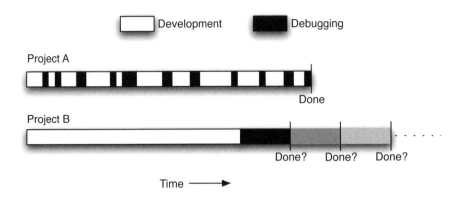

Figure 7.1: DETECTING AND FIXING BUGS EARLY PROVIDES CERTAINTY.

Early Bug Fixing Decreases Uncertainty

Until you start looking for them, you can have little or no idea how many bugs remain to be found. And until you start fixing them, you can't know how long they're going to take to fix. Early bug detection and fixing allows you to *measure* how much of your time you need to spend on bug fixing and adjust your plan accordingly. Late bug fixing, on the other hand, gives you the illusion that you're making progress, but you're just storing up *technical debt*—a backlog of problems lurking under the surface of the software. You can have no idea when you will be done—it's impossible to predict how many more issues are waiting to be found.

We can see this graphically in Figure 7.1. In Project A (at the top), bugs are detected and fixed as soon as possible. As a result, we can measure our true velocity and accurately predict the point where the project is complete (and bug free). By contrast in Project B (at the bottom), we save testing and bug fixing until the end, by which point we have no idea how many outstanding bugs there are or how long they might take to fix. Will we be done next week? Next month? Six months from now? There's really no way to be sure because, even if we knew how much work remained (which we do not), we have no historical data upon which to base our estimate of how long it might take.

Joe Asks...

How Do I Estimate How Long a Bug Will Take to Fix?

In general, it's impossible to estimate how long a particular bug will take to fix. Diagnosis is intrinsically uncertain—any estimate you come up with, until you've resolved that uncertainty, will be of very little value.

Once you've completed your diagnosis, you can probably come up with a good estimate for how long it will take to fix. But that's not likely to be much help because, for the majority of bugs, diagnosis is the most time-consuming element.

All is not lost, however. Although you can't estimate how long a particular bug will take to fix, you *can* make useful statistical statements about a collection of bugs. So, if in the run-up to a release you notice that on average you fixed twenty bugs last week, it's probably reasonable to estimate that you'll do approximately the same in the next week.

Early bug fixing exploits this effect—if we detect and fix bugs as soon as possible, we quickly discover what percentage of our time we need to spend on debugging to achieve bug-free software. Better, we do this without estimating—we simply measure how much time is spent bug fixing.

No Broken Windows

Writing and (particularly) maintaining software is a continual battle against entropy. Keeping on top of quality is tough, requiring high levels of discipline. This discipline is difficult enough to maintain under the best of circumstances, let alone when faced with concrete evidence that the software is uncared for, such as a long-unfixed bug. As soon as discipline slips, quality can go into a self-reinforcing downward spiral, and you're in real trouble.

Problems multiply, and poor quality is contagious—the only sure remedy is to stamp out bugs as soon as they come to light. The goal is to maintain a zero (or as close to zero

Poor quality is contagious.

as possible) bug count at all times. This approach is commonly called *no broken windows*.[1]

Detect bugs early, and do so from day one.

To many of us, jaded by experience of *death-march* projects, a project that successfully follows a "no broken windows" policy can seem an impossible pipe dream. It is definitely possible, however, if you detect bugs early and do so from day one. That way, the number of outstanding bugs (both those you know about and those lurking as yet undetected) never grows out of control.

7.2 The Debugging Mind-Set

As we've already seen, debugging is first and foremost a mental activity. A healthy debugging mind-set can be a difficult balance to strike. Occasionally, it can feel as though you've joined Alice *Through the Looking-Glass* [Car71]:

Alice: *There's no use trying, one can't believe impossible things.*

White Queen: *I daresay you haven't had much practice. When I was your age, I always did it for a half hour a day. Why, sometimes I've believed as many as six impossible things before breakfast.*

Taken naïvely, the "no broken windows" approach could be interpreted to mean that only perfection will do. But as anyone who's ever worked on a nontrivial software project knows, bugs are inevitable. No matter how hard we try, some problems will always slip through the cracks. So, how do we square this circle?

At one end of the spectrum, we could give in to the inevitable, stop worrying, and simply accept that bugs will happen. Although based on a kernel of truth, taken to its ultimate conclusion, this line of reasoning leads to poisonous fatalism—don't worry about the fact that you have bugs; they're a simple fact of life that you can do nothing about. Don't knock yourself out attempting to achieve the impossible; just deal with bugs as and when they arise.

At the other end of the spectrum, as conscientious software developers who aim to both deliver value and take pride in what we do, we want to strive for perfection. Zero tolerance for bugs! Unfortunately, although

---

1. First popularized in the context of software by Andy Hunt and Dave Thomas in *The Pragmatic Programmer* [HT00].

\\// Joe Asks...

Is It a Bug or a Feature?

If you're going to adopt a policy of no broken windows and prioritize all bugs ahead of other development, then you're very quickly going to find yourself having the "is it a bug, or is it a feature?" debate.

From your users' point of view, it's almost entirely meaningless—they just know that what the software is doing is *wrong* and want you to fix it. They're likely to view the bug vs. feature debate in much the same light as the infamous "How many angels can dance on the head of a pin?"

From the no broken windows point of view, however, the distinction is critical. You don't want to allow your carefully considered prioritization of tasks to be subverted by simply redefining features as bugs. Nor do you want to allow quality to slip by miscategorizing bugs as features.

The distinction is, thankfully, relatively clear. Bugs are *unintentional* behavior, where the software isn't behaving according to its design. Anything else, where the software is doing exactly what it's designed to do, is a feature.

Of course, just because the behavior that your users are complaining about is a feature doesn't mean that it doesn't need changing. It just means that it doesn't receive an automatic boost to the head of the queue.

---

well intentioned, this line of reasoning can also end up being unhelpful if taken to its logical conclusion. I've seen it lead to fragile software—why spend time writing software that can fail safe if it's never going to fail in the first place? And it can mean that when the inevitable bugs *do* slip through, we constantly feel as though we've failed. At its worst, this can lead to rancorous witch hunts and a blame culture.

So, if both extremes are unhelpful, where on this continuum should we aim to be?

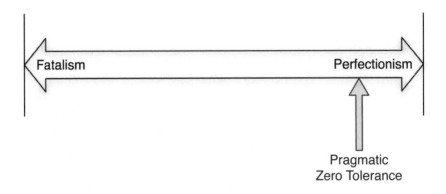

Figure 7.2: PRAGMATIC ZERO TOLERANCE

Temper perfectionism with pragmatism.

The most productive mind-set is *pragmatic zero tolerance*—very close to zero tolerance but tempered with pragmatism (Figure 7.2).

We need to act *as though* bug-free software is an attainable goal—leaving no stone unturned and ignoring no tool or technique that might get us closer. When a bug does slip through the cracks, we should learn as many lessons from it as possible and take whatever action we can to ensure that it doesn't happen again.

But we need to do all this while maintaining a realistic outlook on how close to our ultimate goal we can expect to get. Yes, we should be ruthless in our quest to unearth the cause of any problems but without beating ourselves up when we fall short or trying to apportion blame. And we need to understand that some bugs are inevitable and create software that behaves as robustly as possible in their presence.

It's OK to cut ourselves a little slack, but only a little. Perfection is beyond our reach, but we can get very close with the right approach.

7.3 Digging Yourself Out of a Quality Hole

Occasionally, you're going to find yourself faced with a codebase containing an excess of bugs. Maybe it's a situation that you got yourself into; maybe it's one you inherited. It doesn't matter—if you're faced with a deluge of bugs, how do you get yourself out of the hole?

There Is No Silver Bullet

The sad truth is that there is no quick fix. Although there are strategies available to you that will help, the only sure way out of the problem is to fix all the bugs, and that requires time, effort, and dedication. No shortcuts and no free pass.

From a purist point of view, the obvious solution is to call a halt to proceedings and announce that no new development will take place whatsoever until you are on top of your quality problem. Unfortunately, most organizations don't react well to being told that you're not going to deliver any new features whatsoever for the next six months.

So, what are your options?

Stop the Rot

Your first order of business is to stop things from getting worse. You might not be able to immediately bring all the existing code up to standard, but you *can* ensure that any new code starts out that way.

If you don't already have the basics in place, then your first step should be to put them there—without them, you're simply going to

Put the basics in place.

dig yourself further into the hole you already find yourself in. As a bare minimum, this means the following:[2]

- Source control
- A fully automated build system
- A fully automated test harness
- Overnight builds or continuous integration

Once these are in place, make sure that you use them. You're trying to reverse entropy, and it's not going to be easy to break free from its hold. It's much harder to retrofit quality than it is to build it in from the outset or maintain it.

Separate Clean from Unclean

One challenge you're going to face is that you'll be fighting against the broken windows effect—when you're surrounded by broken windows, it takes a strong effort of will to avoid backsliding.

---

2. We'll cover these in detail in Chapter 9, *The Ideal Debugging Environment*, on page 139.

> ## Boarding Up Broken Windows
>
> In *The Pragmatic Programmer* (HT00), Andy Hunt and Dave Thomas mention that, on occasion, you might consider "boarding up" broken windows:
>
> "If there is insufficient time to fix it properly, then *board it up*. Perhaps you can comment out the offending code, or display a 'Not Implemented' message, or substitute dummy data instead. Take *some* action to prevent further damage and to show that you're on top of the situation."
>
> A variation of this approach is to *sandbox* a problem module. If the code itself is too awful for you to fix with confidence, isolate it as much as you can from the surrounding code. Control its interface so you know exactly how it's being used, and verify the results it returns. Over time, you can eventually excise or rewrite it.

A good strategy can be to clearly demarcate "clean" (well-written, well-tested, and debugged) code from "unclean." Make sure that everyone in the team understands that the clean code must stay that way.

Take the opportunity to move the boundary further into the old code whenever you have an opportunity to do so. If you're working on that code, write tests for any bugs you fix and anything else you touch along the way. After a while, bit by bit, you'll discover that you've incrementally created tests that cover a significant amount of the codebase. At least all of the areas that are currently in flux (which are likely to be the most interesting from a quality standpoint) should end up reasonably well tested.

Bug Triage

Many teams faced with a large and growing bug database choose to put some variety of *bug triage* in place.[3] The purpose of a triage meeting is to review the list of bugs, both old and new, and ensure that you understand their implications and that you have them appropriately prioritized relative to each other.

---

3. Sometimes called a *bug scrub* meeting (in the sense of cleaning your bugs).

These meetings can be the most soul-destroying way to spend time you're likely to find. They tend to go on interminably, and you regularly find yourself having to make impossible trade-offs arising from limited resources.

> Prioritizing bugs requires an overview of the entire bug database.

Nevertheless, if you find yourself in the position where you have a large body of outstanding bugs, it's difficult to see any other way to manage the process. Someone needs to have an overview of the entire database in order to be able to make those difficult trade-offs, and the only way to achieve this is to review that database on a regular basis and ensure that new entries are created with the appropriate priorities.

Worthy of Heroism?
by Bill Karwin

At one job, we developed a metaphor that became a running joke. We were down to the last week of development before shipping our product, and there were still open bugs we had earlier marked top priority. Only some of them could be fixed. I asked the triage team to imagine that our product still has these bugs, and the truck loaded with finished product is rolling away from the loading dock. Do you feel so strongly that these bugs must not get into customers' hands that you'll go down there and lie down in the driveway in front of the truck? It got some laughs, put things in perspective, and helped us decide whether each remaining "top-priority" bug was so important that it would warrant such heroism. In some cases, yes. But in other cases, people had to admit the bug was obscure or else had mild enough consequences.

Bug Blitz

A popular strategy adopted by some teams is to institute a *bug blitz* (sometimes called a *bug fest* or similar). Some relatively short period (a day, a week, or maybe even an iteration) is put aside during which time *everyone* on the team works on nothing but bug fixing.

The object of the exercise is to decrease the number of outstanding bugs as much as possible in the time available, irrespective of their priority. Often, this means the simple bugs—the ones that might otherwise be overlooked as too unimportant—receive time and attention.

Done well, a bug blitz can have both practical and psychological benefits. It can help by simply getting the number of bugs down to a manageable level, helping you see the wood for the trees. And it can give a jaded or demoralized team a sense that they're making progress.

\\// Joe Asks...
.∙.
~ꞓ **How Do I Refactor Untested Code?**

Once you start to get on top of your quality issues, you're going to want to start refactoring the old, crufty, untested code. And you should—the point of the exercise is to clean up problems, and refactoring is a key element of that process.

Remember, however, that refactoring crucially depends upon the support of an extensive suite of automated tests. Without tests, you're not refactoring. You're hacking.

So, how do you refactor untested code? You don't. The first thing you do is write the tests.

It's a technique that needs to be used sparingly and carefully, however. A bug blitz can be fun for a short period—everyone pulling together, the bug count visibly decreasing, shared pizza paid for by the company. But it's fun only for a short period; it can quickly become wearing. We all need to feel as though we're making progress, and nothing but bug fixing for weeks on end will wear anyone down.

You also need to bear in mind that the purpose of a bug blitz is to improve the overall quality. That means you don't get to scrimp on your normal processes—the checks and balances are there for a reason and are just as applicable during a bug blitz.

SWAT Team

A slight variation on the bug blitz is the *SWAT team*—a small team brought together for a limited time for the express purpose of sorting out a specific quality issue.

It's particularly appropriate if you've identified that you have a problem area—a module with an unacceptably high bug count, for example. A typical SWAT team consists of the best, most experienced members of the team who can identify the root cause and bring the right skills and techniques to bear in order to fix the problem once and for all.

In the next part of the book, we'll look at a few special cases that need particular care, how to set up an environment that helps rather than hinders bug fixing, and finally some pitfalls to avoid.

7.4 Put It in Action

- Detect bugs as early as possible, and fix them as soon as they come to light.

- Act *as though* bug-free software was an attainable goal, but temper perfectionism with pragmatism.

- If you find yourself faced with a poor quality codebase, do the following:

    - Recognize there is no silver bullet.

    - Make sure that the basics are in place first.

    - Separate clean code from unclean, and keep it clean.

    - Use bug triage to keep on top of your bug database.

    - Incrementally clean up bad code by adding tests and refactoring.

Part III

Debug-Fu

Chapter 8

Special Cases

Some kinds of bugs benefit from specialized treatment. In this chapter, we'll examine some of these special cases.

8.1 Patching Existing Releases

For excellent reasons, all well-run software projects work to a release schedule. A traditional project might call for one every six months, an Agile project every two weeks, but they both make releases at well-defined, planned, and controlled points.

This process shouldn't be subverted lightly. Nevertheless, on rare occasions you may be faced with a bug so severe that you have no choice but to break from the normal schedule and patch an existing release.

Diagnosing such a bug is no different from any other. The point at which things become tricky is when you start to design your fix, because when designing a patch, your goals are different from normal. Your primary goal is usually fixing the root cause. By contrast, when patching an existing release, it's minimizing risk.

> When patching an existing release, concentrate on reducing risk.

A true fix might involve extensive refactoring or even deep architectural changes. In the absence of the normal checks and balances of the full release process, it's difficult to be certain that these changes won't introduce regressions and end up making things worse rather than better.

As a result, a workaround that addresses the symptoms instead of the root cause can sometimes be the better choice when implementing a patch. This is a very difficult balance to strike—you normally avoid "papering over the cracks" for good reasons.

If you do decide to take this route, don't fall into the trap of assuming that because your fix is a "hack," you can take less care. The converse is true—you need to take *more* care to counteract the potential issues associated with such a fix. Although you can't perform all the checks you normally would for a full release, you should carry out as many as possible. It's at times like this that you really appreciate the effort you've put into automating your test and release process.

The bug will need fixing in the development version too.

As well as patching the current release, you're also going to need to fix the same bug in the development version. You don't want someone using a patched release to upgrade at some point in the future and suddenly discover that whatever problem the patch addressed has come back again. But don't blindly apply the same changes—the development version *will* eventually go through a full release cycle and should, therefore, receive a properly designed fix that addresses the root cause. We will discuss ways in which your source control system can help with this in Section 9.2, *Taming Branches*, on page 145.

Unfortunately, having one fix in the patch and another in subsequent versions raises the specter of incompatible behavior between releases—an issue we'll cover next.

8.2 Backward Compatibility

On the face of it, addressing a bug is a clear-cut process. The behavior should be *this*, but it's actually *that*—just work out why and fix it.

Many bugs are indeed that straightforward. Sometimes, however, if the bug manifests in a version of the software that is already in users' hands, you might need to worry about *backward compatibility*.

The problem is that, if they've been using a version containing the bug for a while, your users may have come to *rely* upon it doing the wrong thing in some way. So, if you fix it without thinking about the consequences, you're likely to have a number of very unhappy users.

> ### ⅋ Joe Asks. . .
>
> #### What If I Need to Patch Existing Releases All the Time?
>
> Patching existing releases is appropriate only under exceptional circumstances. If it's becoming routine, you have a serious problem.
>
> Releasing patches is expensive, dangerous, and wastes time. Doing so continuously leads to thrashing, digging you deeper into the mire. Don't persevere with a broken process—take the time to identify and fix the underlying cause.
>
> - Perhaps the interval between releases is too long? Consider moving to a more Agile process, which will allow you to release more frequently, or creating a maintenance schedule to bring structure to maintenance releases.
>
> - Do you have customers who are "stuck" on old releases? What can you do to get them to upgrade? Perhaps you need to make the upgrade process easier or more reliable? Or remove political constraints (counterproductive upgrade fees, for example)? Or reimplement the key missing feature in version 2.0 that's leading them to stick with 1.4?
>
> - Is your problem simply that you're struggling to cope with an excess of bugs? If so, consider applying the remedies we discussed in Section 7.3, *Digging Yourself Out of a Quality Hole*, on page 108.

Of course, nobody deliberately relies upon broken behavior.[1] Unfortunately, it can be very easy to end up relying upon it accidentally:

- If the bug affects files saved by your application, perhaps your users have built up a collection of corrupt files? Files that won't give the expected results when subsequently opened by an upgraded version of the software? Or even worse, can't be opened at all?

---

1. Apart, perhaps, from crackers exploiting flaws in your software to achieve their nefarious goals.

- If the bug affects your APIs, then any code that interacts with your application might fail when run against a fixed version.

- Fixes that affect the user interface might result in users having to relearn how to operate the software (with associated retraining costs).

Identifying That You Have a Problem

Your first order of business is to determine whether the fix that you're working on is likely to have compatibility implications. Unfortunately, this can be tricky—users can come to rely on all sorts of subtleties, and it's very difficult to predict what they might be.

Asking them directly is very unlikely to bear fruit—such dependencies are almost always accidental and, therefore, unconscious.

Add identifying compatibility issues to your bug-fixing checklist.

Your primary tool is simply thinking about the change you're considering in the context of your understanding of the big picture to see whether you can think of any way in which it might cause compatibility issues. To that end, it can make sense to have this as one of the items on your bug-fixing checklist as a prompt to make sure that it's not forgotten.

Your regression test suite can sometimes help with identifying backward compatibility issues. Unfortunately, hand-constructed tests tend to be simple, exercising a simple use case, whereas the kinds of problem we're trying to identify here tend to depend upon complex interactions between loosely connected areas of the software. So, it's an excellent idea to build up a library of "real-world" examples collected from the field that you can use for this purpose. The wider the range of such examples in your library, the more likely you are to identify problems before they reach the outside world.

Addressing Compatibility Issues

Once you've determined that the fix you're working on might cause compatibility problems, what can you do about it?

You're looking to find a balance between two potentially antagonistic goals. On the one hand, you want to implement a high-quality fix for the problem. On the other, you want to minimize any pain caused by

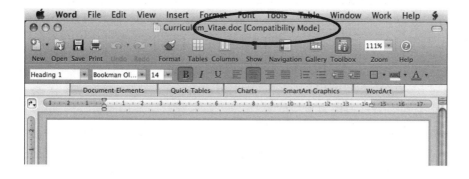

Figure 8.1: MICROSOFT WORD'S COMPATIBILITY MODE

a lack of backward compatibility. Unfortunately, achieving both simultaneously might be impossible—you may end up looking for the best compromise.

A range of options are open to you.

Provide a Migration Path

Give your users some way to modify their existing data, code, or other artifacts to fit in with the new order, such as a utility that converts existing files so they work correctly with the new software, for example.

It might be possible to automate this so that data is automatically upgraded during installation. Make sure that you both test this carefully and save a backup, though—your users will not thank you if the upgrade fails and destroys all their data in the process.

Implement a Compatibility Mode

Alternatively, you can provide a release that contains both the old and new code, together with some means of switching between them. Users can start by using the *compatibility mode*, which runs the old code, and switch to the new after they've migrated. Ideally this switch is automatic—when the software detects an old file, for example.

Microsoft Word is a good example of this approach. When it opens an old file (with a .doc extension), it does so in a compatibility mode (see Figure 8.1). Save that file in the new format (.docx), and Word's behavior, and possibly your document's layout, changes.

A compatibility mode is an expensive solution.

This is not a solution to be adopted lightly. It's very high cost, both for you and for your users. From your point of view, it does nothing for the quality of the code. From the user's point of view, it's confusing—they need to understand that the software supports two different behaviors, what the differences are, and when each is appropriate. Turn to it only if this cost is truly justified.

If you're lucky, you will need to support compatibility code only for a limited time (one or two releases maybe) to provide your users with a grace period during which they can migrate. After that, you can clean the code up again. That's nice in theory, but these things have a habit of "sticking"—you will be able to clear out your compatibility code only if you successfully persuade your users to migrate. And why should they when everything is working fine?

Provide Forewarning

If you know that you're going to have to make a significant change but don't have to make it immediately, you can provide users with forewarning that they will eventually need to migrate. Sun, for example, does this frequently when it deprecates Java APIs.

Of course, this works only if you can afford to delay your fix for long enough to enable your users to migrate—and whether your users *do* migrate.

Don't Fix the Bug

The final option is to leave the bug in place—the pain of fixing the associated compatibility issues might outweigh the advantages of fixing it.

This isn't a palatable solution, but very occasionally it might be the pragmatic choice.

It's Not Just *Your* Bugs You Need to Worry About

PostScript is a *Page Description Language* used (among other things) to control printers. The language was created by Adobe Systems, but several third parties have developed their own implementation. Back in the early 90s, I worked on one of them.

There was a test suite widely used at the time that consisted of thousands of reference pages occupying several meters of shelf space.[2]

---

2. Shelves that were above my desk and that almost killed me one day when the shelf supports collapsed!

The problem was that these reference pages had to be generated by a real implementation (in this case Adobe's), and, like any sizable software system, it contained the occasional bug. So, when there was a discrepancy between what our software produced and the test suite, occasionally it wasn't our bug.

In theory.

The point of a printer is to create output. Customers aren't interested in philosophical debates about why their pages don't match their expectations—it prints fine on *that* printer, so why does the one running your software get it wrong? So in a number of cases, we decided that the pragmatic approach was to emulate the bugs in the reference implementation. It's not pretty maybe, but that's the way the world works sometimes.

8.3 Concurrency

Concurrent software can be a rich source of difficult-to-reproduce, difficult-to-diagnose, and difficult-to-fix problems. Bugs in such software often exhibit nondeterminism, depend upon subtle and difficult to understand interactions, and suffer from mysterious failure modes.

Simplicity and Control

You can build a number of things into your concurrent software that will help during debugging. The two keys are *simplicity* and *control*.

Simplicity is a key element of any software design, but it's particularly valuable when dealing with concurrency. Keep the interactions between independent threads straightforward, and constrain them to as small a number of areas of code as possible. You might be surprised how simple you can make the interactions.

The Simplest Thing That Could Possibly Work

We were designing a server that, when eventually deployed, would have to handle thousands of concurrent requests. These threads needed to share data, accessing and modifying it concurrently.

The shared data took the form of a tree, and we debated the merits of various ways of providing safe concurrent access to it for a long time. We had grand plans in which different subtrees could be locked for reading or writing and schemes to avoid the danger of deadlock in the event of threads requiring multiple simultaneous locks. It was all very clever, but was it necessary?

> Eventually, we created a harness that simulated thousands of users accessing the server and ran some load tests. It turned out that a single "multiple-reader, single-writer" lock was more than adequate for the kind of access patterns we envisaged. This simplified things dramatically—you can't have deadlock with a single lock.

Not only does a simple design make your software easier to understand and less likely to contain bugs in the first place, it also makes it easier to control—which is particularly useful when trying to reproduce problems in concurrent software. If your threads interact with each other only in a few well-defined ways and at a few well-defined places, then it's much easier to ensure that they always interact in exactly the way that you want them to during debugging.

Most bugs in concurrent software are perfectly "normal" and have nothing to do with the fact that it's concurrent. But having to deal with multiple threads during diagnosis can complicate things considerably. As a result, it's particularly useful to build in the option to be able to run the software with no concurrency whatsoever—either by restricting it to a single thread or by forcing threads to run serially in a well-defined sequence (instead of context switching at the whim of the scheduler).

Most bugs that *are* related to the concurrent nature of the software reproduce only if context switches occur at very specific places and times. Reliably reproducing the bug depends upon accurately controlling exactly when these context switches take place. As we saw in Section 2.5, *Multithreading*, on page 31, sometimes you can achieve this with judicious use of sleep( ), but it's much preferable to build the ability to control exactly what order things happen in into your synchronization code.

Fixing Concurrency Bugs

There is one key thing to remember when you come to fixing bugs in concurrent software—making them less likely to happen is *not* an acceptable fix.

Often you will find that there's a specific "window" in which a race condition can arise. It might be easy to see how to make the window smaller, but not so easy to see how to close it entirely.

For example, you might launch a number of threads at approximately the same time and find that if their initialization code runs simultaneously, then you can end up with problems. An obvious, but incorrect, fix would be to stagger launching the threads on the assumption that by the time the second thread is starting, the first will have finished its initialization.

The problem with any fix of this nature is that if a window isn't completely closed, sooner or later your software *will* fall into it. Except that now it will do so only under unusual circumstances (perhaps when the system is heavily loaded and running more slowly than normal). All you've managed to do is make it even harder to reproduce and track down the next time.

In particular, sleep() is almost never the right way to go. As we've already discussed, it can be fantastically useful as a means of forcing a bug to reproduce reliably or to test a theory

> Avoid usingsleep() when fixing concurrency bugs.

about how the software is behaving, but it is not the right tool for fixing concurrency bugs. Think of it as the **goto** of concurrent programming— if you find yourself considering it, that is a red flag.

8.4 Heisenbugs

A *heisenbug*—a bug that "goes away" the instant you start looking for it—is so named by analogy with the *Heisenberg Uncertainty Principle* from quantum mechanics, which (loosely speaking) states that it's impossible to observe a system without changing its behavior.[3] The typical heisenbug reproduces reliably in the field but goes into hiding the instant you start looking for it. They can be very frustrating to diagnose.

The problem is that all the techniques available to you to examine your software's behavior affect that behavior to some degree or another. Whether you capture the information you need by adding instrumentation directly to the code or by running it under a debugger, doing so will almost certainly change its timing, its layout in memory, or both.

For most bugs, this doesn't matter, but a heisenbug relies on some nondeterministic aspect of your software. This in itself can be a useful clue. As you recall from Section 2.5, *Make Nondeterministic Bugs Deterministic*, on page 29, nondeterminism can arise only from a very limited range of causes, so the fact that you're faced with a heisenbug means that it must in some way or another be affected by one of them.

---

3. This is more correctly known as the *Observer Effect*—the Heisenberg Uncertainty Principle actually relates to the accuracy with which we can perform measurements of quantum mechanical systems. But it's a cute name, so pedantry be damned.

The quickest and easiest thing to try is to switch from one method of collecting information to another. If you tried running the software under the debugger, try adding instrumentation directly to the source, or vice versa. The simple fact that the effect of the debugger is different from that of direct instrumentation may be all you need.

Minimize the side effects of collecting the information you need.

If your luck isn't with you, then your task becomes finding some way to gather the information you need that affects the software with a sufficiently light touch as to leave its behavior unchanged.

Logging is a prime source of timing changes—calling System.out.println(), for example, takes thousands of clock cycles and probably involves at least one context switch.

You can use your knowledge of which areas might be the source of nondeterminism to avoid affecting those areas. If, for example, the code contains a tight loop in which it interacts with another thread, there's a good chance that affecting the timing of the loop will change its behavior. Remove any instrumentation you've added to the loop, and see whether your bug comes out of hiding. If it does, then see whether you can find a way to collect the information you need without affecting its timing too heavily.

In-Memory Logging

Some years ago, when working on a large multithreaded product, I found myself trying to track down a particularly slippery heisenbug. We had plenty of logging scattered throughout the code that had repeatedly proven its value in diagnosing thread synchronization issues. Unfortunately, the instant I switched it on, the code behaved flawlessly.

I didn't want to lose the logging, because I was pretty sure that it would tell me what I needed to know. If only I could find a way to reduce its impact on the code's execution.

The solution was to reimplement the log functions so that instead of using the normal output functions, they wrote to large in-memory buffers (one for each thread, so I didn't need to worry about synchronizing access to a shared buffer). These buffers were output after the sensitive portion of the code had finished executing and subsequently interleaved (so that log messages appeared in the right order).

Although clearly the new logging functions still had *some* effect, this turned out to be small enough that the problem now reproduced. And as I hoped, the output gave me exactly what I needed to identify its cause.

Joe Asks...

How Can I Be Certain That I've Fixed a Heisenbug?

The fact that a heisenbug seems to fade in and out of existence as readily (and as frustratingly) as the Cheshire Cat can make it particularly difficult to be sure that you really have fixed it. If you can make the bug "go away" by simply running the software under a debugger or adding a single output statement, then who's to say that your fix isn't just triggering the same disappearing act?

The only solution is to be even more careful than normal to be certain that you really understand the underlying root cause. If there's any doubt whatsoever, err on the side of caution, and assume that you've only masked, not fixed, it.

Say, for example, you determine that the bug is caused by an uninitialized variable and fix it by initializing it to NULL. Don't stop there—*how*, exactly, does the fact that the variable was uninitialized cause the behavior you observed? Could it ever take that value? If you explicitly initialize it to this "bad" value, do you see what you expect?

8.5 Performance Bugs

Donald Knuth's famous pronouncement that "premature optimization is the root of all evil"[4] should be etched in the mind of every professional software engineer. More bad code has been written in the misguided pursuit of efficiency than any other cause.

But that doesn't mean that you can ignore efficiency. If your software is taking ten minutes to perform a task it should be performing in ten seconds, then you definitely have a problem.

Find the Bottleneck

As with any kind of bug, the key to solving a performance problem is identifying the root cause. And nine times out of ten, what that means is that you're looking to find the *bottleneck*—the particular area of the code that is restricting overall performance.

---

4. From *Structured Programming with go to Statements* [Knu74].

In most software, a small minority of the code accounts for a large majority of the execution time. Your first task is to identify where the software is spending all of its time. Once you have done so, then you can move on to work out why.

> **Profile your code before diagnosing a performance bug.**

For this reason, one tool stands head and shoulders above all others when tracking down performance bugs—the *profiler*.

Profilers vary in the details of how they work (some require specific hooks to be compiled in, for example, whereas others operate against unmodified code) and in the amount of detail they generate. What they all have in common is that they examine your code as it executes to generate a report (or profile) of where it's spending most of its time. This is invaluable data—after you've tracked down a few performance bugs, you will quickly discover that predicting bottlenecks by examining the code is virtually impossible. The only way to be sure is to act on real data gathered from running software.

Your main concern, therefore, is to ensure that the profile you generate accurately reflects your software's true behavior.

Accurate Profiling

The Observer Effect applies to profiling just as much as any other means of observing your code—the simple fact that you're looking at its performance will, theoretically at least, change the very thing you're trying to examine. Knowing this, the authors of such tools have invested a huge amount of effort to ensure that they affect the software they're profiling as little as possible. So, in most cases, you don't have to worry about the profiler itself skewing the results of your investigation.

Far more likely to adversely affect the quality of your results is how you build and run your software. You need to make sure of the following:

- You profile a build that is as close as possible to a production release. In particular, make sure that you build it with the same level of optimization.

- The environment you run in is as similar as possible to the software's ultimate target environment. The machine you use for development might, or might not, fit this bill depending upon the variety of software you develop.

> ## Joe Asks...
> ### What If There Is No Bottleneck?
>
> Occasionally, instead of there being one or a handful of bottlenecks, the software is just "generally slow," or the slowdowns seem to happen in random places at random times. In that case, you need to start looking for things that can affect the software's performance holistically. Prime candidates include the following:
>
> Resource exhaustion: Is the operating system having to page in order to satisfy your software's memory requirements? Do you have a memory or other resource leak? Are you suffering from memory fragmentation?
>
> Garbage collection: If your software allocates a lot of short-lived objects, the garbage collector may have to run very frequently.
>
> Caching: If your software implements or relies upon some kind of cache (memory, disk, or otherwise), are you getting an excessive number of cache misses?

- You run the software with representative data. It can be tempting, for example, to run with small data sets because they're more convenient than real production data, but this can generate misleading profiles (perhaps overemphasizing the effect of tasks that represent a constant overhead or failing to bring caching or paging effects to light).

8.6 Embedded Software

Debugging embedded software can be particularly tricky, not because it's complicated or involved (although it can be) but because of the environment it runs within. Embedded systems typically run on hardware that is very different from your development environment, with limited performance and facilities, which can make gaining access to the information required for efficient debugging very difficult indeed.

Embedded Debugging Tools

A number of specialized tools have evolved to help:

⌣/ Joe Asks...
How Do I Detect Performance Regressions?

Performance regressions can sneak into software very easily—as we've already seen, predicting software's performance by inspection is very difficult and so is predicting the performance implications of changes.

It is an excellent idea, therefore, to incorporate performance tests into your regression test suite. They might run representative operations on large data sets and report if the time taken falls outside of acceptable bounds, for example.

It can even be worth having tests that fail when things become unexpectedly *faster*. If a test suddenly runs twice as fast after a change that shouldn't have affected performance noticeably, that can also indicate a problem. Perhaps some code you were expecting to be executed isn't any longer?

Emulation: Emulators and simulators vary in sophistication and the precise details of how they work (some, for example, run the same binary as the target hardware, and others require a slightly different build), but they all have the same goal—allowing you to run and debug your software on your development machine instead of having to use the target hardware. By simplifying and shortening the edit/build/test cycle, they can save you a huge amount of time and effort. In addition, they provide enhanced access to information difficult to obtain from the production hardware.

Remote debugging: Many embedded environments provide support for remote debugging. The target hardware is connected to a development machine (via a serial cable, network connection, or similar), and the debugger runs on the development machine and controls the embedded system.

Development hardware: A development board is a version of the target hardware designed for development purposes. It will have additional interfaces and possibly support test facilities such as error simulation. One of the major benefits of development hardware is that it often provides built-in support for an in-circuit emulator.

Joe Asks...

Is It a Hardware Problem or a Software Problem?

One of the challenges of developing embedded software is that it often takes place in parallel with the development of the hardware it's going to run on. There is an unfortunate tendency when there's a problem for the hardware guys to blame the software guys, and vice versa.

Whatever the rights and wrongs of the matter, it's typically much harder to fix a problem in hardware than it is to find a way to work around it in the software. So, whether or not it's "your" problem, you're likely to be the person fixing it.

In-circuit emulator (ICE): In-circuit emulation is a somewhat over-loaded term, but in general an ICE is a debugger that uses a combination of hardware and software to provide detailed access to the internals of an embedded system. These days many systems have standardized on the JTAG interface, which (among other things) provides a standard means of accessing the debugging features present in embedded hardware.

These tools are invaluable, but they aren't always available (sadly, supporting the poor software developer tends to be close to the bottom of the hardware guys' to-do list), so on occasion you're likely to find yourself having to cope with primitive or nonexistent debugging facilities. And sometimes, even if they are available, the bug you're chasing will reproduce only on the production hardware.

Extracting Information the Hard Way

Given its limited facilities, the major challenge of debugging a problem directly on the target hardware is often getting access to the information you need. A little imagination, however, and you can normally find some way to communicate it.

The system you're working on is controlling *something*. You can use that control as a communication channel. Perhaps there's an LCD display you can use? Or a serial port you can write to?

> **One bit is enough.**

It doesn't have to be a rich channel—one bit is enough. Is there an LED you can light up? Or a motor you can run? Getting information out this way isn't convenient, but it *is* possible.

The Logic Analyzer As a Software Debugging Tool

I was working on the device driver for a printer. It was working just fine, most of the time. But occasionally the output was getting corrupted. The code was very simple, just taking a bitmap and feeding it out to the printer piecemeal. I couldn't see how it could be corrupting the data en route.

Eventually we reasoned that the cause might be a timing problem—perhaps the device driver wasn't responding to interrupts fast enough? But how could we measure accurately enough to confirm our theory?

The solution turned out to be a *logic analyzer*, a hardware-debugging tool that displays signals within digital circuits. I modified the device driver to raise a signal on an unused interface line at the end of its interrupt routine, and we connected the logic analyzer to that line. By triggering the analyzer when the interrupt was raised, we could accurately measure the interval between the interrupt and it being handled successfully.

Sure enough, most of the time the interrupt was being handled in plenty of time. But every once in a while it was being delayed long enough for things to go wrong. By moving the point at which the device driver raised a signal on the line we were monitoring, we could accurately pinpoint exactly where the delay was occurring.

The solution wasn't easy—it turned out to be caused by the operating system's virtual memory architecture and required a lot of effort to address. But at least we knew what we were up against.

8.7 Bugs in Third-Party Software

The days of self-contained software are long gone. Modern software has to interface with a diverse array of code written by third-parties—building upon libraries and frameworks, consuming data provided by servers, and providing data to clients in turn.

Sooner or later, you're going to be faced with a bug that is (or appears to be) within something you didn't write, don't control, and may not have source for. Handling this kind of bug brings its own unique challenges.

Don't Be Too Quick to Point the Finger

Third-party code is just code. And like any code, it can contain bugs. So yes, it's quite possible that the problem you're trying to track down isn't of your own making.

But beware—it's very easy to point the finger of blame too eagerly.

Most of the third-party code you're likely to interface with is going to be used in many more products or by many more people than yours. That means it's been well tested, and most of the more obvious bugs have already been found.

Three Months Getting Nowhere
by Dave Strauss

One member of our team had been working on a bug full-time for more than three months. He ended up spending a lot of time trying to understand the inner workings of a fairly complicated third-party library and getting nowhere.

And then a colleague fixed the problem in half a day almost by accident—he needed to use the feature that was affected by the bug, and he noticed that (for the particular case he was interested in) the library was being invoked incorrectly.

I talked to him afterward, and he told me that what he did was make the assumption that the library basically worked, which led him to examine how it was being used, and the answer just "jumped out" at him. He said that assuming the library worked was pretty safe because this code was widely distributed and used in many places.

Treat your own code with suspicion. Start by assuming that's where the bug is. If you eventually conclude that the bug is elsewhere, go back to your own code *again* and look harder. Only blame third-party code when you really have exhausted all other avenues.

Suspect your own code first.

Dealing with Bugs in Third-Party Code

If you *have* found a bug in third-party code, you need to work out what to do about it. You may have no choice other than to report it and wait for the author or vendor to fix it for you, but you may be able to find a workaround for the problem.

Or, if you have access to the source code, you might even be able to fix it yourself. But that raises the question of whether you *should*.

> ### Reporting Bugs in Others' Code
>
> You can dramatically improve the chances of getting a bug in third-party code fixed if you do a good job of reporting it. Think carefully about what you would want to see in a bug report if you were in their shoes. Make sure that it meets the criteria in Section 6.1, *What Makes a Good Bug Report?*, on page 90.
>
> Remember that all code has bugs. No doubt you're frustrated at the time that it's taken you to track down the problem, and as a result, you may not feel well-disposed toward the author. Keep that frustration out of your communication, stick to the constructive and factual, and you're much more likely to make progress.

Why wouldn't you fix the problem yourself if you have the option? Bug fixes are supposed to address the underlying cause, aren't they?

Think carefully before using your own patched version of third-party code.

Under normal circumstances, yes. But a bug in third-party code isn't the normal case. The problem with any modification you make to third-party code, including bug fixes, is that you're now working with something different from everyone else. That is likely to cause you problems if you need support and, particularly, when upgrading to a new release—reapplying your custom fix is an error-prone process raising the specter of regressions.

The best solution is often, therefore, to work around the problem in the short-term and get your fix incorporated into the official release in the long-term. How easy this is depends in large part upon who owns the code and what your relationship with them is like.

Open Source

An increasingly important category of third-party code is open source.

Linus' Law

Many believe that open source changes debugging fundamentally. This argument was most famously made by Eric S. Raymond in *The Cathedral and The Bazaar* [Ray01] in which he coins *Linus' Law*—"Given enough eyeballs, all bugs are shallow."[5]

> Given enough eyeballs, all bugs are shallow.

This may indeed be true for open source projects on the scale of Linux. But there are a colossal number of open source projects and a limited number of eyeballs. So, open source won't mean the end of traditional debugging any time soon.

The Open Source Build Process

Everything we've discussed so far applies to open source development as much as any other approach, but there are a couple of issues that are particularly pertinent—build configuration and reporting.

The nature of open source means that you aren't going to be able to build the software centrally. Anyone can build it at any time they choose, and the computer they build it on is going to differ from yours in significant ways. It's going to be built on different operating systems, with varying compilers, library versions, and configurations. You're not going to be able to control this, but you *can* make sure that you automate the build process as completely as possible (avoiding "finger trouble" on the part of whoever is building the software) and that you collect all the information necessary to allow you to understand, and if necessary replicate, the environment in which it was built.

For good examples of this, take a look at Firefox's about:buildconfig page (Figure 8.2, on the next page) or the results of passing the -V command-line option to the Apache HTTP Server.

Participating in the Community

One of the great things about open source communities is that they are so wonderfully helpful. Not only can you get high-quality software completely free, but often technical support of an equally high quality is also freely available.

---

5. More formally, "Given a large enough beta-tester and codeveloper base, almost every problem will be characterized quickly, and the fix will be obvious to someone."

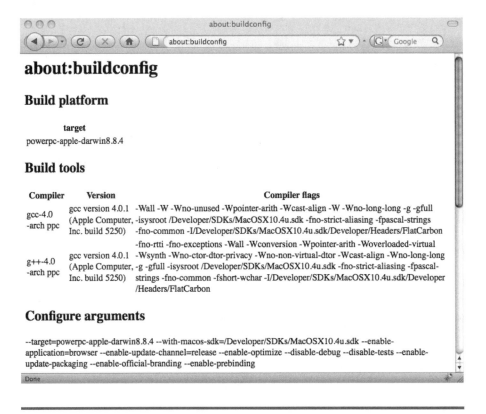

Figure 8.2: FIREFOX'S ABOUT:BUILDCONFIG PAGE

But there's an art to asking for help effectively:

- Do your due diligence first. Check the documentation and frequently asked questions, and search mailing lists and blog entries to see whether anyone else has encountered the same problem.

- Give as much information as possible. What have you tried already, what results are you seeing, and why are you expecting to see something different?

- Remember that open source community members are typically volunteers. If they choose to help you out, as they probably will, that's their decision.

If you rely upon open source, then you owe the other members of the community to contribute what you can. Participate in Linus' Law by reporting and characterizing bugs. If you fix a bug, then submit the fix back to the central distribution. Contribute documentation, tutorials, and examples, and answer others' questions on mailing lists and forums.

8.8 Put It in Action

- When patching an existing release, concentrate on reducing risk.

- Keep on the lookout for compatibility implications when fixing bugs.

- Ensure that you have completely closed any timing windows, not just decreased their size.

- When faced with a heisenbug, minimize the side effects of collecting information.

- Fixing performance bugs always starts with an accurate profile.

- Even the most restricted communication channel can be enough to extract the information you need.

- Suspect your own, ahead of third-party, code.

Chapter 9

The Ideal Debugging Environment

Debugging doesn't take place in a vacuum. By taking the time to make sure that the basics are in place before you're faced with a bug, you can save yourself a huge amount of time, effort, and frustration when you do face one.

In this chapter, we'll discuss these basics:

- A fully automated test harness
- Source control
- A fully automated build system
- Overnight builds or continuous integration

9.1 Automated Testing

As we've already discussed, agile software development has dramatically changed software construction through the widespread adoption of automated testing and refactoring. We looked at refactoring in Section 4.4, *Refactoring*, on page 71; in this section, we'll cover testing.

Effective Automated Testing

There's more to effective automated testing than simply automating your tests. To achieve maximum benefit, your tests need to satisfy the following goals:

Unambiguous pass/fail: Each test outputs a single bit—pass or fail. No shades of gray, no qualitative output, no interpretation required. Just a simple yes or no.

Self-contained: No setup required before running a test. Before it runs, it sets up whatever environment it needs automatically, and just as important, it undoes any changes to the environment afterward, leaving everything as it found it.

Single-click to run all the tests: All tests can be run in one step without interfering with each other. As with a single test, the output of the complete test suite is a simple pass or fail—pass if every test passes, fail otherwise.

Comprehensive coverage: It's easy to prove that achieving complete coverage for any nontrivial body of code is prohibitively expensive. But don't allow that theoretical limitation to put you off—it is possible to achieve close enough to complete coverage as to make no practical difference.[1]

Automated Tests as an Aid to Debugging

So, what makes automated tests valuable when debugging? They help out at all stages:

- First and foremost, well-tested code tends to have fewer bugs in the first place. The easiest bug to fix is the bug that never existed.

- The shorter the delay between a mistake being made and subsequently being discovered, the easier and cheaper it is to fix. Early testing means that most bugs are discovered very shortly (often immediately) after they're introduced.

- Automated testing is a key enabler of continuous integration, in which code is integrated with the whole product as soon as it's complete. We'll discuss this further later in this chapter.

- Automated tests allow you to frequently release new versions of the software with high confidence that the new release is functional. This means that you get end-user feedback on new features and bug fixes much more quickly than would otherwise be the case (again, reducing the time between code being written and bugs being discovered within the code). It can also reduce the need to back-port bug fixes to previous versions of the software or to release patches.

---

1. Testing "everything that could possibly break" in XP parlance.

- For code to be tested, it needs to be structured in such a way as to provide access to intermediate results and internal state that might otherwise be unavailable. This kind of access turns out to be a great help during later debugging.

- Writing a test is an excellent way to reproduce a bug during the diagnostic process. Many of the techniques created to support automated testing are extremely useful for reliably reproducing bugs.

- After you've completed your diagnosis, automated tests provide powerful protection against the fix introducing regressions.

- If, during diagnosis, you make a habit of always writing a test that reproduces the bug, you naturally end up with a regression test that ensures that the bug won't be reintroduced at some point in the future.

- Automated tests are a key enabler of refactoring, which is the most powerful weapon at your disposal to ensure that code remains well-structured and flexible throughout its lifetime.

Automated tests are a particularly powerful debugging tool when allied with a technique that has risen in popularity alongside them—test doubles.

Mocks, Stubs, and Other Test Doubles

Test doubles are "pretend" objects used in place of the real object during a test. There are several kinds of test double, most commonly *mock objects* and *stubs*.

Mocks and stubs are often confused. Stubs are passive, simply responding with canned data when called, whereas mocks are active, validating expectations about how and when they are called. For a detailed description of the difference, see Martin Fowler's *Mocks Aren't Stubs* [Fow].

> Mocks are active; stubs are passive.

For our purposes, test doubles are most useful when we're trying to reliably reproduce a bug in which interaction with some other portion of the system is important.

Consider, for example, a Java class (which fetches data from a server over the network) with the following interface:

```java
public interface DataServer {
  boolean connect(String serverAddress);
  String fetchItem(int itemId);
  void disconnect();
}
```

Imagine that we've found a bug in code that calls this, which occurs only if fetchItem() raises a SocketTimeoutException on the third time it's called. Reproducing this bug by pulling the network cable out of the back of our computer at *just* the right moment is not likely to be an efficient way to proceed.

Instead, we can create a stub that simply returns exactly the right data to invoke the bug:

```java
public class StubDataServer implements DataServer {
  public boolean connect(String serverAddress) {
    return true;
  }
  public String fetchItem(int ItemId) {
    switch(itemId) {
      case 1: return «Data item 1»; break;
      case 2: return «Data item 2»; break;
      case 3: throw new SocketTimeoutException("Timeout from stub");
    }
  }
  public void disconnect() {
  }
}
```

Note that StubDataServer is really "dumb." If it's used anywhere other than in a test that we're using to reproduce this specific bug, nothing good will happen.[2] But that doesn't matter—what we've created will be used only in this specific context and doesn't need to operate elsewhere.

9.2 Source Control

A source control or configuration management system is a repository that keeps track of your source code, together with a history of all of the changes that have been made to it over its lifetime. Other than your

---

2. Contrast this with Section 10.2, *Debugging Subsystems*, on page 169 in which we discuss a technique that can be used more generally.

compiler or interpreter, it's probably the single most important tool at your disposal.

From a debugging standpoint, source control helps across the board. It's a key element of a controlled build process that ensures that you know *what* you're debugging and that you're running exactly the same code as the user. During diagnosis, it can pinpoint the precise change that introduced the bug and help you keep track of the experiments you've tried. When you come to implement your fix, it ensures that you make only the changes you mean to and, in concert with your continuous integration server (we'll cover continuous integration later in this chapter), that they work as intended.

Most of the tricky issues with source control are related to *branching*. Branching is a means by which we can support parallel development of more than one version of a piece of software at a time. There are two common reasons why this might be necessary—*stabilization* and *maintenance*.

Stabilization

Imagine that we're working on version 2.0 of a widely used desktop application. Things have been going well, and we've gotten to a point where we think we have something almost ready for release. Many teams in this situation implement some form of *change freeze*—a moratorium on checking in any changes that might destabilize the software while it goes through the final stages of the release life cycle (such as alpha and beta testing). Often this means something like "only critical bug fixes." For some projects, this period can last several months.[3]

This makes perfect sense, but what if we want to make a start on features we expect to ship in version 2.1 while we're waiting for 2.0 to stabilize and ship?

A common answer is to create a *release branch*—a copy of the source from which the 2.0 release will be made. Any changes we need to make before release go into this branch, and in the meantime development can proceed unhindered in the trunk. For a graphical representation of release branches, see the left side of Figure 9.1, on the following page.

---

3. When Firefox 3 when through this process, for example, Beta 1 was released in November 2007, the first release candidate was released in May 2008, and the final release took place in the following month.

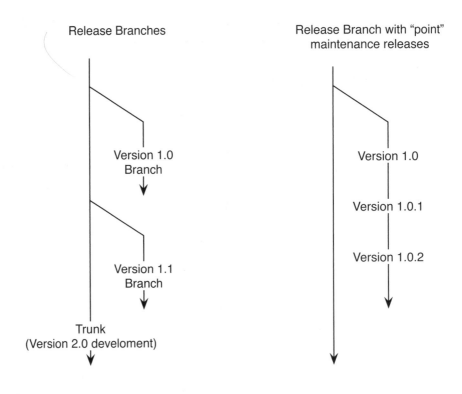

Release Branches

Release Branch with "point" maintenance releases

Version 1.0
Branch

Version 1.0

Version 1.0.1

Version 1.1
Branch

Version 1.0.2

Trunk
(Version 2.0 develoment)

Figure 9.1: BRANCHES

Maintenance

The release went well, many happy users are enjoying 2.0, and we're making good progress with the exciting new features we're going to wow them with in 2.1. Life is good.

And then the bug report arrives—there's a critical problem with 2.0 that absolutely has to be fixed. What to do?

Well, we certainly can't make a release from the trunk, because we've made extensive changes to it—changes that haven't yet been through enough testing for us to trust them "in the wild." This is where the release branch we made during stabilization proves its worth a second time, as a *maintenance branch.*

We fix the bug in the branch, increase the version number to 2.0.1, and life is good again. For a graphical representation of point releases on a maintenance branch, see the right side of Figure 9.1.

This all sounds simple enough, so why is it that the subject of branching causes battle-weary software engineers to blanch?

The Problem with Branches

Branching results in duplicate work. Every time we fix a problem in the branch, we almost certainly need to make the same—or worse, a similar but different—change in the trunk. If we don't, then we're going to end up with a regression when we release the next version. If we have more than one branch active, we might even have to make it in other branches as well.

> Branching results in duplicate work.

Merging changes made in one branch into another is difficult to understand and error prone, especially if the branches have diverged significantly. What's more, there's a temptation to skimp on the testing of the merged fix—after all, we've already tested it in the branch we're merging from, so testing it again in the trunk is wasted time, surely? And it is, right up until the unforeseen problem bites us.

Support for branching in source control systems varies considerably, both in terms of how branches are implemented (some behave as though the source had been copied, whereas others treat branches as a different "view" of a single copy) and how well branches are supported. They can be difficult to understand, even when you've been using them for a long time.[4] The interface often leaves a lot to be desired, and they can interact in surprising ways with other source control features.[5]

As a result, it's not unusual for changes that should have been merged to be forgotten or for changes to merge badly, breaking the build or introducing regressions. In general, branches tend to consume a lot of time, effort, and emotional energy.

Taming Branches

The best solution to the previous is not to branch at all. But this isn't always possible—sometimes branches are a necessary evil.

---

4. I've lost track of how many times I've drawn a "How branches work in Subversion" diagram on the whiteboard while explaining them to a member of my team—often to the same person I was explaining it to a couple of months ago.

5. External items in Subversion, for example, aren't branched when the project they're included within is branched.

\\// Joe Asks...
~
Are There Any Other Reasons to Use Branches?

Stabilization and maintenance aren't the only valid use cases for branches—they can also be useful during exploration and collaboration.

A private branch can be very useful if you want to safely "play" with some potentially destructive changes. Or a branch can provide a means by which two or more developers can exchange code and collaborate on something that's not (yet) ready to be part of the main system.

Branches created for these purposes are different from those created for stabilization and maintenance because they're ad hoc and (should be) short-lived. You should worry if they hang around for too long because they can provide a "back alley" through which code can bypass important elements of your process.

A number of rules of thumb will help minimize the pain, however:

- Branch as late as possible. It may be tempting to create your stabilization branch well in advance (after all, if some stabilization is good, more must be better?), but the chances are that the productivity you lose by doing so isn't worth it.

- Stick to a single level of branching. If you find yourself branching your branches, you know that you're in trouble.

- Set up your continuous integration server to build all the branches that are actively being worked on.

- Check in small changes often. Small changes are easier to understand, merge, and roll back if necessary.

- Make only those changes that *really* need to be in the branch in the branch.

- Merge from the branch to the trunk, not the other way around. The branch represents released software, so a problem in the branch is likely to have more severe consequences than a problem in the trunk.

- Merge changes from the branch into the trunk immediately. This ensures that the merge isn't forgotten and that you do it while the change is fresh in your memory. Don't collect several changes and merge them all at once.

- Keep an audit trail so that you know which changes have been merged and when (not all source control systems do this for you automatically).

Source control becomes particularly powerful when allied with the next technique we're going to cover—an automated build process.

9.3 Automatic Builds

One the most important variables you need to control during debugging is the software itself. You need to be able to identify and re-create the same software in which the bug manifests. Specifically, you need to control the following:

- The source that the software is built from

- The tools used to build it

- The options passed to those tools at build time

- Any third-party libraries linked or shipped with the software

Building modern software can be an involved process utilizing many different tools that need to be invoked in a specific order and manner. Some teams choose to address this by having a long "How to build ProjectXYZ" document. A much better solution is to encode all this knowledge in software as part of an automated build process.

The One-Button Build

What you're aiming for is a "one-button" build process. You know that you've succeeded when a new developer can join your team, check out the source onto a completely virgin machine, run a single command, and end up with a fully built version of the product that is identical to that built by the established members of the team.

Plenty of tools exist to help you achieve this (Maven if you're working in Java, say, or Boost.Build if you're working in C++—see Section A.2, *Build Tools*, on page 197 for more). If your software follows a reasonably standard architecture, you may be lucky and discover that these tools give you everything you need out of the box. If not, you may find yourself

> ### ⚡ Joe Asks...
> #### What About My IDE's Build System?
>
> The value of an automated build system is significantly reduced if it isn't used by everyone on the team. Sometimes developers might prefer the build system provided by their choice of IDE, for example.
>
> Most IDEs can call out to an external build, so see whether you can integrate your automatic build system that way. If not, spend time making it as slick as possible so it's just as easy to use as the integrated system. Alternatively, some IDEs now support a sophisticated enough build system that, if every member of the team is happy to use the same IDE, you could use it as the basis for your automatic build.
>
> The team needs to agree how to build the software and stick with it—if different developers build in different ways, it's only a matter of time before you hit problems.

having to write custom rules. The time you spend doing so will repay itself many times over—even one manual step is one too many.

Automate your entire build process, from start to finish.

Your system should automate the process all the way through to whatever you're going to finally release. If your software is packaged into an installer, building that installer should be automatic. If you record what you've built with a tag in source control, creating that tag should be automatic. You may not perform these steps every time you run a build (when building on your own machine during development, for example), but that just makes automation more important—the things you do infrequently are precisely those you're likely to get wrong.

Build Machine

Your automated build process *should* guarantee that everyone gets exactly the same result whenever they build. But developers' machines tend to be in flux—we have local modifications to the source for new features we're writing, or we have new versions of build tools we're experimenting with.

When making a release, it's important that everything is in a well-known state, which can be difficult and error prone to achieve on a development machine. So, it's a good idea to have a build machine that is used to make release builds (possibly several build machines if you're working on cross-platform software). It should always be kept pristine and not be used for anything else so that you can trust that it's in the right state.

Never release software built on a developer's machine.

A build machine is worth having, but you can increase its value to the team immeasurably by taking the next step and turning it into a continuous integration server.

Continuous Integration

Some points in the software development life cycle are intrinsically higher risk than others. One of the riskiest is when integrating (supposedly) independent changes made by different members of the team. Everything works just fine when you test your changes locally but breaks when you integrate your changes with everyone else's.

This is where your build machine becomes worth its weight in gold as a *continuous integration server*. Every time any changes are checked into source control, it automatically checks them out, builds them, and runs the entire test suite (a typical continuous integration system is shown in Figure 9.2, on the next page). If the build or any of the tests fail, it sends a mail message to the team so that the problem can be fixed ASAP.

Run your tests every time you change the software.

A number of very nice continuous integration server packages are available (see Section A.2, *Continuous Integration Tools*, on page 198 for a list), but given a good automated build system, creating one for yourself is very easy, so don't be put off if you need to roll your own.

Versioning

So, the bug report tells you that it manifests in 3.6.209(e3). Great. Now what does that tell you?

It's useful information only if you can identify *exactly* what went into building it, which means tying the version number to source control. Therefore, whenever you make a release, you need to make sure that you keep a record of what source was used to create that release.

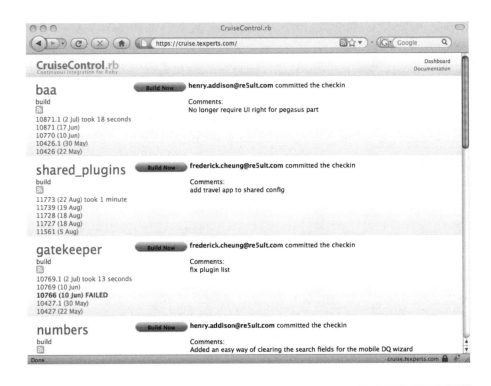

Figure 9.2: A CONTINUOUS INTEGRATION SERVER

Depending upon the source control system you're using, this might mean creating a tag, a branch, a label, or something else. Whatever mechanism you use, you need to ensure that there is a one-to-one relationship between version numbers and source.

Different source, different version number. This has a very important corollary—*never reuse a version number*. If, immediately after you release something, you discover a critical bug and need to make another release to fix it, change the version number for the new release. This applies no matter how small the change is—different source, different version number.

Static Analysis

Much of debugging relies upon *dynamic analysis*—examining the software as it executes. But it turns out that many bugs can be identified just by examining the source code statically. Even better, this kind of static analysis can be automated, integrated into your development

---

\\// Joe Asks...
;\f
≥ __What About an Overnight Build and Smoke Test?__

Some teams use an overnight build and smoke test (named after the test that hardware engineers perform when they flip the power switch for the first time—does the hardware expire with a puff of magic blue smoke?). Microsoft famously used this approach in the development of Windows NT, as described in *Show-stopper!* (Zac94).

As you might imagine, continuous integration and an overnight build and smoke test have much in common and convey many of the same advantages. Under normal circumstances, continuous integration is preferable (why integrate only overnight if you can do so continuously?), but if your test suite takes a prohibitively long time to run, then overnight may be your only choice.

If you do have problems with tests that take too long to run, consider creating a suite of short tests that you can run for every check-in, as well as running the full suite overnight.

---

process, and used to detect bugs before you've even executed the code once.

If you've spent any time reading someone else's code, you will know that some bugs "leap out at you." There are certain patterns that, although they're *legal* code, almost certainly aren't what the author meant to write.

Here's a simple Java example—can you spot the bug in the following?

```
if(«first condition» &&
  «second condition» ||
  «third condition»);
{
  «some code»
}
```

Anyone who's ever worked in a C-like language (C, C++, Java, C#, and the rest) will have been bitten by this at some point. If you haven't seen it yet, the problem is the semicolon after the **if** condition, which means that the following block will *always* be executed, whatever the condition evaluates to.

Don't Forget the Compiler

Before you start hunting for new tools, don't forget your humble compiler. Over the years, modern compilers have acquired a slew of warnings that, in some cases, can even put dedicated static analysis tools to shame.

The trick is that often they're not enabled by default. So, don't assume that just because your code compiles warning-free right now, there aren't lurking issues that the compiler could dig out for you. Take the time to read your compiler's documentation—often you will find that there are some useful warnings that have to be enabled separately. GCC's -Wall option, for example, which you might naïvely assume would enable *all* warnings, actually leaves many very useful ones disabled. You can enable a wider set with -Wextra, but even that leaves a number you might want to enable separately.

It turns out that there are lots of patterns of code that experience tells us are, to some degree, questionable. Other simple examples include unreachable code (which can never be executed, whatever state the program is in) and unused variables (which are declared, possibly even written to, but never read from). In the following Java method, for example, the variable at ❶ is unused, and the code at ❷ is unreachable:

```java
public static boolean allUpper(String s) {
❶    int length = s.length();

    if (s == null) {
      return false;
❷      System.out.println("Null string passed to allUpper");
    }

    CharacterIterator i = new StringCharacterIterator(s);

    for (char c = i.first(); c != CharacterIterator.DONE; c = i.next())
      if (Character.isLowerCase(c))
        return false;

    return true;
}
```

One interesting case is when we accidentally write code that depends upon undefined behavior. Many language specifications contain dark corners where it's possible to write what seems to be perfectly sensible code, where in fact it's impossible to predict what its behavior will be. Here's an example in C++ (a language replete with dark corners):

```
int x = 1;
x = x++;
// What value does x have here?
```

The answer is that x could have *any* value whatsoever—the C++ standard simply doesn't define what this code does. In practice, most compilers will do something "sensible" with it, and typically x will end up equal to either 1 or 2. But theoretically speaking, it could end up equal to 42, the program could crash, or anything else could happen. That, unfortunately, is what undefined means.

Interestingly, if you compile the same code in Java, then its behavior *is* defined—x will always end up with the value 1. But don't feel too smug if you're a Java developer—the behavior may be defined, but it's still almost certainly a bug. Presumably whoever wrote this code intended it to do *something*, where in fact it's a no-op. So, whatever it was they intended it to do, it's not doing it.

Just about every language has a number of tools available that crawl over your code looking for exactly this kind of problem. The granddaddy of them all is lint, which was finding bugs in C programs back in the 70s, to the extent that *lint* has become a generic term for any tool of this nature.

Using Static Analysis

The great thing about static analysis is that it gives us a way to detect bugs almost for free. Instead of waiting for a bug to manifest (either during testing or in the field) and then going through the long process of reproduction, diagnosis, and fix, we can simply run our code through one of these tools and address the problems it finds. What's not to like?

So, the first rule is to *use* static analysis. Switch on all of the warnings supported by your compiler and get hold of any other tools that might prove useful in your environment.

The second rule is to integrate your chosen tool or tools tightly into your development process. Don't run them only occasionally—when you're looking for a bug, for example. Run

Integrate static analysis into your build process.

\\// Joe Asks...

How Do I Become Warning Free?

If you're starting a new project from scratch, writing warning-free code is easy. But if you're starting from an existing code-base, it can be much less straightforward. The chances are that the first time you increase your compiler's warning level or run a new tool, you will disappear under a tidal wave of warnings. Often these result from systemic issues with the code—common mistakes you've made over and over again, which have gone unnoticed until now, but each instance of which generates a warning. There are also issues that tend to "percolate" through the code generating many warnings (const-correctness in C++ is a classic example).

The solution is to be pragmatic. Most static analysis tools provide fine-grained control over which warnings are generated where (via comments embedded in the source code, for example). Very often you can get the number down to a manageable level by switching off the one or two warnings that account for the majority or by excluding a "problem" module. You can go back and fix these other warnings at a later date, but you gain most of the benefit of static analysis in the interim.

The same approach can help on the rare occasions where a buggy tool generates spurious warnings for legitimate code, where you knowingly choose to write "questionable" code, or where a third-party library generates warnings.

them every single time you compile your source. Treat the warnings they generate as errors, and fix them immediately.[6]

This chapter has covered a number of techniques that are external to the software. But there are others that are built into the software itself. These are the subject of the next chapter.

---

6. Most compilers provide an option to treat warnings as errors, such as -Werror for GCC, for example.

9.4 Put It in Action

- Automate your tests, ensuring that they do the following:

    - Unambiguously pass or fail

    - Are self-contained

    - Can be executed with a single click

    - Provide comprehensive coverage

- Use branches in source control sparingly.

- Automate your build process:

    - Build and test the software every time it changes.

    - Integrate static analysis into every build.

Chapter 10

Teach Your Software to Debug Itself

Plenty has been written about how to write good software. Much less has been written about how to create software that is easy to debug.

The good news is that if you follow the normal principles of good software construction—separation of concerns, avoiding duplication, information hiding, and so on—as well as creating software that is well structured, easy to understand, and easy to modify, you will also create software that is easy to debug. There is no conflict between good design and debugging.

Nevertheless, you can put a few additional things in place that will help when you find yourself tracking down a problem. In this chapter, we'll cover some approaches that can make debugging easier or even, on occasion, unnecessary:

- Validating assumptions automatically with assertions

- Debugging builds

- Detecting problems in exception handling code automatically

10.1 Assumptions and Assertions

Every piece of code is built upon a platform of myriad assumptions—things that have to be true for it to behave as expected. More often than not, bugs arise because one or more of these assumptions are violated or turn out to be mistaken.

Joe Asks. . .

Do I Need Assertions If I Have Unit Tests?

Some people argue that automated unit tests are a better solution to the problem that assertions are trying to solve. This line of thought probably arises to some extent from the unfortunate fact that the functions provided by JUnit to verify conditions within tests are also (confusingly) called *assertions*.

It isn't a question of either/or but of both/and. Assertions and unit tests are solving related but different problems. Unit tests can't detect a bug that isn't invoked by a test. Assertions can detect a bug at any time, whether during testing or otherwise.

One way to think of unit tests is that they are (in part) the means by which you ensure that all your assertions are executed regularly.

It's impossible to avoid making such assumptions and pointless to try. But the good news is that not only can we verify that they hold, we can do so automatically with *assertions*.

What does an assertion look like? In Java, they can take two forms—the first, simpler form is as follows:

```
assert «condition»;
```

The second form includes a message that is displayed if the assertion fails:

```
assert «condition» : «message»;
```

Whichever form you use, whenever it's executed, an assertion evaluates its condition.[1] If the condition evaluates to true, then it takes no action. If, on the other hand, it evaluates to false, it throws an AssertionError exception, which normally means that the program exits immediately.

So much for the theory; how does this work in practice?

An Example

Imagine that we're writing an application that needs to make HTTP requests. HTTP requests are very simple, comprising just a few lines of

---

1. If assertions are enabled, which we'll get to soon.

text. The first line specifies the method (such as GET or POST), a URI, and which version of the HTTP protocol we're using. Subsequent lines contain a series of key/value pairs (one per line).[2] For a GET request, that's it (other requests might also include a body).

We might define a small Java class called HttpMessage that can generate GET requests as follows:[3]

```java
public class HttpMessage {

    private TreeMap<String, String> headers = new TreeMap<String, String>();

❶  public void addHeader(String name, String value) {
        headers.put(name, value);
    }

❷  public void outputGetRequest(OutputStream out, String uri) {
        PrintWriter writer = new PrintWriter(out, true);

        writer.println("GET " + uri + " HTTP/1.1");
        for (Map.Entry<String, String> e : headers.entrySet())
            writer.println(e.getKey() + ": " + e.getValue());
    }
}
```

It's very simple—addHeader() ❶ just adds a new key/value pair to the headers map and outputGetRequest() ❷ generates the start line, followed by each key/value in turn.

Here's how we might use it:

```java
HttpMessage message = new HttpMessage();

message.addHeader("User-Agent", "Debugging example client");
message.addHeader("Accept", "text/html,text/xml");

message.outputGetRequest(System.out, "/path/to/file");
```

That will generate the following:

```
GET /path/to/file HTTP/1.1
Accept: text/html,text/xml
User-Agent: Debugging example client
```

So far, so simple. What could possibly go wrong?

Well, our code is very trusting. It's just taking what it's given and passing it through as is. This means that if it is called with bad

---

2. See the Hypertext Transfer Protocol [iet99] specification for further details.
3. Of course, you wouldn't write this code yourself given the number of well-debugged HTTP libraries available. But it's a nice simple example for our purposes.

\\/
·,· **Joe Asks...**
ᔔ   <u>**How Do I Choose a Good Assert Message?**</u>

An early reviewer of this book spotted a poster in, of all places, Google's Beijing offices that read, "Make sure that your error messages aid in debugging and don't just tell you that you need to debug."

The example that they cited was an assertion of the general form:

```
assert_lists_are_equal(list1, list2);
```

If this fails, it tells you that the lists are not equal. You still have to go through the code trying to find where the lists started to differ. It would be better to highlight the first element where the difference occurs, whether the order has changed, or something else that gives you a head start diagnosing the problem.

arguments, it will end up generating invalid HTTP requests. If, for example, addHeader() is called like this:

```
message.addHeader("", "a-value");
```

then we'll end up generating the following header, which is sure to confuse any server we send it to:

```
: a-value
```

We can automatically detect whether this happens by placing the following assertion at the start of addHeader():

```
assert name.length() > 0 : "name cannot be empty";
```

Now, if we call addHeader() with an empty string, when assertions are enabled, the program exits immediately with this:

```
Exception in thread "main" java.lang.AssertionError: name cannot be empty
    at HttpMessage.addHeader(HttpMessage.java:17)
    at Http.main(Http.java:16)
```

Wait a Second—What Just Happened?

Let's take a moment to reflect on what we've just done. We may have added only a single, simple line of code to our software, but that line has achieved something profound. We've taught our software to debug itself. Now, instead of us having to hunt down the bug, the software itself notices when something is wrong and tells us about it.

Ideally this happens during testing, before the embarrassment of it being discovered by a user, but assertions are still helpful when tracking down bugs reported from the field. As soon as we find a way to reproduce the problem, there's a good chance that our assertions will immediately pinpoint the assumption that's being violated, dramatically saving time during diagnosis.

Example, Take Two

Now that we've started down this road, how far can we go? What other kinds of bugs can we detect automatically?

Detecting empty strings is fair enough, but are there any other obviously broken ways in which our class might be used? Once we start thinking in this way, we can find plenty.

For a start, empty strings aren't the only way that we could create an invalid header—the HTTP specification defines a number of characters that aren't allowed to appear in header names. We can automatically ensure that we never try to include such characters by adding the following to the top of addHeader():[4]

```
assert !name.matches(".*[\\(\\)<>@,;:\\\"/\\[\\]\\?=\\{\\} ].*") :
    "Invalid character in name";
```

Next, what does the following sequence of calls mean?

```
message.addHeader("Host", "somewhere.org");
message.addHeader("Host", "nowhere.com");
```

HTTP headers can appear only once in a message, so adding one twice has to be a bug.[5] This is a bug that we can catch automatically by adding the following to the top of addHeader():

```
assert !headers.containsKey(name) : "Duplicate header: " + name;
```

---

4. Don't worry too much about the hairy regular expression in this code—it's just matching a simple set of characters. It looks more complicated than it might because some of the characters need to be escaped with backslashes, and those backslashes themselves also need to be escaped.

5. Note to HTTP specification lawyers—I am aware that there are occasions where headers can legitimately appear more than once. But they can always be replaced by a single header that combines the values, and for the sake of a simple example, I'm choosing to ignore this subtlety.

Other checks we might consider (depending on exactly how we foresee our class being used) might include the following:

- Verifying that outputGetRequest() is called only once and that addHeader() isn't called afterward

- Verifying that headers we know we always want to include in every request are always added

- Checking the values assigned to headers to make sure that they are of the correct form (that the Accept header, for example, is always given a list of MIME types)

So much for the example—are there any general rules we can use to help us work out what kind of things we might assert?

Contracts, Pre-conditions, Post-conditions, and Invariants

One way of thinking about the interface between one piece of code and another is as a *contract*. The calling code promises to provide the called code with an environment and arguments that confirm to its expectations. In return, the called code promises to carry out certain actions or return certain values that the calling code can then use.

It's helpful to consider three types of condition that, taken together, make up a contract:

Pre-conditions: The pre-conditions for a method are those things that must hold before it's called in order for it to behave as expected. The pre-conditions for our addHeader() method are that its arguments are nonempty, don't contain invalid characters, and so on.

Post-conditions: The post-conditions for a method are those things that it guarantees will hold after it's called (as long as its pre-conditions were met). A post-condition for our addHeader() method is that the size of the headers map is one greater than it was before.

Invariants: The invariants of an object are those things that (as long as its method's pre-conditions are met before they're called) it guarantees will *always* be true—that the cached length of a linked list is always equal to the length of the list, for example.

If you make a point of writing assertions that capture each of these three things whenever you implement a class, you will naturally end up with software that automatically detects a wide range of possible bugs.

Switching Assertions On and Off

One key aspect of assertions that we've already alluded to is that they can be disabled. Typically we choose to enable them during development and debugging but disable them in production.

In Java, we switch assertions on and off when we start the application by using the following arguments to the java command:

```
-ea[:<packagename>...|:<classname>]
-enableassertions[:<packagename>...|:<classname>]
            enable assertions
-da[:<packagename>...|:<classname>]
-disableassertions[:<packagename>...|:<classname>]
            disable assertions
-esa | -enablesystemassertions
            enable system assertions
-dsa | -disablesystemassertions
            disable system assertions
```

In other languages, assertions are enabled and disabled using other mechanisms. In C and C++, for example, we do so at build time using conditional compilation.

Why might we choose to switch them off? There are two reasons—efficiency and robustness.

Evaluating assertions takes time and doesn't contribute anything to the functionality of the software (after all, if the software is functioning correctly, none of the assertions should ever do anything). If an assertion is in the heart of a performance critical loop or the condition takes a while to evaluate (thinking back to our earlier example, an assertion that involved parsing the HTTP message to check that it's well-formed), it is possible to have a detrimental effect on performance.

A more pertinent reason for disabling assertions, however, is robustness. If an assertion fails, the software unceremoniously exits with a terse and (to an end user) unhelpful message. Or if our software is a long-running server, a failed assertion will kill the server process without tidying up after itself, leaving data in who-knows-what state. Although this may be perfectly acceptable (desirable in fact) when we're developing and debugging, it almost certainly isn't what we want in production software.

Instead, production software should be written to be *fault tolerant* or to *fail safe* as appropriate. How you go about achieving this is outside the scope of this book, but it does bring us onto the thorny subject of *defensive programming.*

Defensive Programming

Defensive programming is one of the many terms in software development that means different things to different people. What we're talking about here is the common practice of achieving small-scale fault tolerance by writing code that operates correctly (for some definition of correctly) in the presence of bugs.

Software should be robust in production and fragile when debugging.

But defensive programming is a double-edged sword—from the point of view of debugging, it just makes our lives harder. It transforms what would otherwise be simple and obvious bugs into bugs that are obscure, difficult to detect, and difficult to diagnose. We may want our software to be as robust as possible in production, but it's much easier to debug *fragile* software that falls over immediately when a bug manifests.

A common example is the almost universal **for** loop idiom, in which, instead of writing this:

```
for (i = 0; i != iteration_count; ++i)
    «Body of loop»
```

we write the following defensive version:

```
for (i = 0; i < iteration_count; ++i)
    «Body of loop»
```

In almost all cases, both loops behave identically, iterating from zero to iteration_count - 1. So, why do so many of us automatically write the second, not the first?[6]

The reason is because if the body of the loop happens to assign to i so that it becomes larger than iteration_count, the first version of our loop won't terminate. By using < in our test instead of !=, we can guarantee that the loop will terminate if this happens.

The problem with this is that if the loop index *does* become larger than iteration_count, it almost certainly means that the code contains a bug. And whereas with the first version of the code we would immediately

---

6. Actually, this idiom is starting to fall out of favor in the C++ community thanks to the Standard Template Library, but nevertheless there are millions of examples in existence.

ASSUMPTIONS AND ASSERTIONS ◀ 165

notice that it did (because the software hung inside an infinite loop), now it may not be at all obvious. It will probably bite us at some point in the future and be very difficult to diagnose.

As another example, imagine that we're writing a function that takes a string and returns *true* if it's all uppercase and *false* otherwise. Here's one possible implementation in Java:

```java
public static boolean allUpper(String s) {
    CharacterIterator i = new StringCharacterIterator(s);

    for (char c = i.first(); c != CharacterIterator.DONE; c = i.next())
        if (Character.isLowerCase(c))
            return false;

    return true;
}
```

That's a perfectly reasonable function—but if for some reason we pass null to it, our software will crash. With this in mind, some developers would add something along these lines to the beginning:

```java
if (s == null)
    return false;
```

So, now the code won't crash—but what does it *mean* to call this function with null? There's an excellent chance that any code that does so contains a bug, which we've now masked.

Assertions provide us with a very simple solution to this problem. Wherever you find yourself writing defensive code, make sure that you protect that code with assertions.

So, now our protective code at the start of allUpper() becomes the following:

```java
assert s != null : "Null string passed to allUpper";
if (s == null)
    return false;
```

And our earlier **for** loop becomes the following:

```java
for (i = 0; i < iteration_count; ++i)
    «Body of loop»
assert i == iteration_count;
```

We now have the best of both worlds—robust production software and fragile development/debugging software.

> ### Assertions and Language Culture
>
> A programming language is more than just syntax and semantics. Each language has one or more communities built up around their own idioms, norms, and practices. How (or if) assertions are habitually used in a language depends in part on that community.
>
> Although assertions can be used in any language, they are more widespread in the C/C++ community than any other of the major languages. In particular, they aren't particularly widely used in Java, probably because they became only officially supported in Java 1.4 (although there are signs that assertions are catching on within the wider Java community with JVM-based languages such as Groovy and Scala encouraging their use).
>
> In part, this may be because there are more opportunities for things to go wrong in C/C++. Pointers can wreak havoc if used incorrectly, and strings and other data structures can overflow. These kinds of problems simply can't occur in languages like Java and Ruby.
>
> But that doesn't mean that assertions aren't valuable in these languages—just that we don't need to use them to check for this kind of low-level error. They're still extremely useful for checking for higher-level problems.

Assertion Abuse

As with many tools, assertions can be abused. There are two common mistakes you need to avoid—assertions with side effects and using them to detect errors instead of bugs.

Cast your mind back to our HttpMessage class, and imagine that we want to implement a method that removes a header we added previously. If we want to assert that it's always called with an existing header, we might be tempted to implement it as follows (the Java remove() method returns null if the key doesn't exist):

```
public void removeHeader(String name) {
    assert headers.remove(name) != null;
}
```

The problem with this code is that the assertion contains a *side effect*. If we run the code without assertions enabled, it will no longer behave correctly because, as well as removing the check for null, we're *also* removing the call to remove().

Better (and more self-documenting) would be to write it as follows:

```
assert headers.containsKey(name);
headers.remove(name);
```

An assertion's task is to check that the code is working as it should, not to affect *how* it works. For this reason, it's important that you test with assertions disabled as well as with assertions enabled. If any side effects have crept in, you want to find them before the user does.

Assertions are a bug detection mechanism, not an error-handling mechanism. What is the difference? Errors may be undesirable, but they *can* happen in bug-free code. Bugs, on the other hand, are impossible if the code is operating as intended. Here are some examples of conditions that almost certainly should not be handled with an assertion:

> Assertions are not an error-handling mechanism.

- Trying to open a file and discovering that it doesn't exist

- Detecting and handling invalid data received over a network connection

- Running out of space while writing to a file

- Network failure

Error-handling mechanisms such as exceptions or error codes are the right way to handle these situations.

We've mentioned that assertions are typically disabled in production builds and enabled in development or debug builds. But what exactly is a debug build?

10.2 Debugging Builds

Many teams find it helpful to create a *debugging build*, which differs from a release build in various ways designed to help reproduce and diagnose problems.

\\// Joe Asks...

> **But Aren't Debugging Builds Different?**

Compiler writers go to great lengths to ensure that switching optimization off, or additional checks on, doesn't change behavior. And if you care about preserving your nerves, you'll do the same for your assertions and logging.

But the simple truth of the matter is that a debugging build is different from the production build. Most of the time it won't matter, but bear it in mind. If you have problems getting a bug to reproduce in the debug build, try the production build instead.

Compiler Options

Most compilers provide you with a wide range of options that allow you to control exactly how they translate your source code into object code. Often it makes sense to use a different set of options during development and debugging from those used in production. Here are a few examples:

Optimization: Modern compilers can perform wonders, generating object code that is as efficient, or better, than hand-rolled machine code. In the process of doing so, however, they often restructure things so much that the relationship between source code and object code can become muddied. This can, for example, make single-stepping in a debugger confusing or even impossible. As a result, debug builds often disable optimization.

Debugging information: To be able to single step through the source, debuggers need to know how to map lines of source code to regions of object code. Typically these are excluded from a production release because they add size and may give away information we would rather keep to ourselves.

Bounds checking: Some C/C++ compilers provide an ability to add bounds checking to arrays and other data structures.

There's more to a debugging build than just choosing different compiler options, however.

Debugging Subsystems

Sometimes it's worth thinking about replacing an entire subsystem with a version specifically designed to make debugging easier. This can be particularly useful if we can't easily control the behavior of the production version of the subsystem (because it's under the control of a third-party, for example, or because its behavior has some random element).

Imagine, for example, that our software interfaces with a server provided by a third-party and we're trying to debug a problem that occurs only when it returns a specific sequence of results. It may not be easy, or even possible, to find a way to ensure that it always returns that exact sequence on demand. Even if we can, its owners may not thank us for bombarding it with requests—especially if those requests aren't well-formed (which is likely to be the case during debugging).

There is some overlap between a debugging subsystem and the test doubles we discussed earlier in Section 9.1, *Mocks, Stubs, and Other Test Doubles*, on page 141. The difference is one of *scale* and *scope*. A test double is a short-lived object only intended for use within a single test. A debugging subsystem is normally a complete replacement for its associated production subsystem, implementing all of its interfaces and operating correctly across a wide range of use cases. It may even make sense for us to ship a debugging subsystem with the software so that end users can enable it in order to help us debug a problem in situ.

A debugging subsystem either can entirely replace its corresponding production system (emulating its entire behavior) or can be implemented as a shim that sits between the rest of the software and the production system, modifying its behavior as appropriate.

One particular subsystem you might want to consider bypassing during debugging is the user interface.

Solving the User Interface Problem

The needs of the end user and the needs of a developer are often very different. A graphical or web-based user interface might make it very easy for end users to achieve their goals, but it can get in the way during development and debugging because such interfaces are difficult to control programmatically.

> ## Joe Asks. . .
> ### What If I'm Using an Interpreted Language?
>
> The same general principle—that it's occasionally appropriate for our software to behave differently during development and debugging from production—holds no matter what language it's written in, whether compiled or interpreted. The mechanism by which this is achieved will have to be at runtime in an interpreted language, however, given that conditional compilation isn't an option.

For this reason (among others), it makes sense to ensure that the user interface layer is as thin as possible, just looking after the details of displaying information and soliciting input from the user. In particular, it should contain no business logic whatsoever. This should mean that you can replace it with an alternative such as a scripting language that can drive the rest of the software, which is likely to be much easier to work with from a debugging standpoint.

This might fall out in the wash if your software implements an *object model* such as (OLE) Automation under Windows or AppleScript support on the Mac. It might even be worth adding support for such an object model exclusively for debugging.

Another subsystem commonly replaced with a debugging version is the memory allocator.

Debugging Memory Allocators

In languages like C and C++, which don't provide automatic memory management, a debugging memory allocator can be worth its weight in gold. A debugging allocator can help you detect and solve a number of common problems:

- By keeping track of memory allocation and deallocation, it can detect memory leaks (memory that is allocated but not freed).

- By placing *guards* before and after allocated memory, it can detect buffer overflows and memory corruption.

- By filling memory regions with known patterns, it can detect instances where memory is used without being initialized.

> ## Memory Integrity Checkers
>
> A debugging memory allocator requires that you modify your object code to use it. *Memory integrity checkers* are tools that can perform a similar analysis on any program by using the processor's virtual memory architecture.
>
> Personally speaking, I prefer to use a debugging allocator because it typically works at a more fine-grained level, giving you greater control and insight. But an integrity checker can prove useful if you find yourself having to debug a problem that shows up only in a production build or when working with a legacy application.
>
> There is a list of such tools in Section A.4, *Runtime Analysis Tools*, on page 201.

- By filling deallocated memory with a known pattern and holding onto it, it can detect instances where memory is written to after it has been deallocated.

For a list of debugging allocators, see Section A.3, *Debugging Memory Allocators*, on page 198.

Built-in Control

As well as modifying the behavior of third-party code, we can also choose to have our own code behave differently in a debug build, building in the control that will prove useful during diagnosis. Examples include the following:

Disabling features: Sometimes your software might include features that are valuable in production but obfuscate things during debugging. Communication between one part of the application and another might be encrypted for security reasons, for example. Or data structures might be optimized to improve memory usage and execution speed. You are likely to make problems in these areas much easier to diagnose if you allow such features to be selectively disabled.

Providing alternative implementations: Sometimes there is more than one way to implement a module—one that is simple and easy to understand and another that is complex and optimized. By including both within the code and providing a means to switch between them, you can validate the results of the complex version against the simple one. This can help pinpoint whether the bug resides in the optimized version or elsewhere, and it can help with debugging even if it does lie elsewhere by making things simpler to understand.

Although we tend to talk about two different builds, debug and release, there's nothing to stop you from building other flavors. Many teams, for example, have an *integration* build that acts as a halfway house between a debug and a release build. It might, for example, have debugging symbols and assertions enabled like a debug build but have optimizations enabled like a release build.

10.3 Resource Leaks and Exception Handling

It's always a good idea to do everything you can to detect problems early rather than wait until they surface in production. But this is particularly true for some classes of problem, foremost among which are resource leaks and exception-handling bugs.

> Don't wait for resource leaks to manifest— detect them automatically and early.

These problems tend to be related (resource leaks often arise from incorrect exception handling) and tend to be *systemic*. If you make a mistake in one place, you're very likely to make the same mistake elsewhere. Wait until the symptoms come to light, and you're going to find yourself faced with a massive task—by that time, the code will be riddled with problems.

Happily, both types of problem can be detected automatically. In this section, we'll look at an example of how to do so in C++, although the same general approach can be applied to any language.

Automatically Throwing Exceptions in Tests

The approach builds upon two widely used tools—a debugging memory allocator and a unit test framework. We're going to create our own very simple unit test framework that adds one new facility—the ability to indicate points at which an exception might be thrown. Each test is then run multiple times. The first time it's run as normal, and the test framework simply keeps a record of which exceptions might be thrown.

It's then run again, once for each possible exception, and that exception is thrown.

This is useful anywhere an exception might be thrown, but there's one particular place that's especially appropriate—whenever memory is allocated. Our example overrides global operator new() and operator delete() as follows:

```
void* operator new(size_t size) {
    TEST_ERROR(bad_alloc());
    void *p = malloc(size);
    if(!p)
        throw bad_alloc();
    return p;
}

void operator delete(void *p) {
    free(p);
}
```

❶

The key is the call to TEST_ERROR() on line ❶, which lets the test framework know that operator new() might throw a bad_alloc exception. We'll look at the implementation of TEST_ERROR() later. For the time being, let's see how this helps us debug our exception handling.

An Example

Imagine that we're writing a class that implements a simple binary tree. Here's a first attempt:

```
class TreeNode {
public:
    TreeNode(int value) : m_value(value), m_left(0), m_right(0) {}
    ~TreeNode() {
        delete m_left;
        delete m_right;
    }

    int value() const { return m_value; }
    TreeNode* left() const { return m_left; }
    TreeNode* right() const { return m_right; }

    void setLeft(TreeNode* left) { m_left = left; }
    void setRight(TreeNode* right) { m_right = right; }

private:
    int m_value;
    TreeNode* m_left;
    TreeNode* m_right;
};
```

The implementation is simplicity itself—each TreeNode maintains an integer value together with pointers to its left and right subtrees. A few simple getter and setter functions and we're done.

We can test that everything is working as expected by creating a simple test function:

```
void testTree() {
    auto_ptr<TreeNode> root(new TreeNode(42));
    assert(!root->left());
    assert(!root->right());

    root->setLeft(new TreeNode(10));
    assert(root->left()->value() == 10);
    assert(!root->right());

    root->setRight(new TreeNode(20));
    assert(root->left()->value() == 10);
    assert(root->right()->value() == 20);
}
```

And this is what running the test might look like:

```
Running test: testTree
    exception run: 1
    exception run: 2
    exception run: 3
```

In total, the test runs four times—the first time is the "normal" run, followed by three further runs, one for each memory allocation.

So far, so good. Now, let's get a bit more adventurous and implement a copy() method that copies an entire tree. That shouldn't be too hard, should it?

```
TreeNode* copy() {
    TreeNode* node = new TreeNode(m_value);
    if(m_left)
        node->m_left = m_left->copy();
    if(m_right)
        node->m_right = m_right->copy();
    return node;
}
```

Looks simple enough.

Let's see what happens when we add a call to it at the end of our test:

```
Running test: testTree
    exception run: 1
    exception run: 2
    exception run: 3
    exception run: 4
    exception run: 5
Memory leaks found during test: testTree(5)
0 bytes in 0 Free Blocks.
12 bytes in 1 Normal Blocks.
0 bytes in 0 CRT Blocks.
0 bytes in 0 Ignore Blocks.
0 bytes in 0 Client Blocks.
Largest number used: 0 bytes.
Total allocations: 48 bytes.
    exception run: 6
Memory leaks found during test: testTree(6)
0 bytes in 0 Free Blocks.
24 bytes in 2 Normal Blocks.
0 bytes in 0 CRT Blocks.
0 bytes in 0 Ignore Blocks.
0 bytes in 0 Client Blocks.
Largest number used: 0 bytes.
Total allocations: 60 bytes.
```

I guess that implementing an exception-safe version of copy() isn't as easy as it seemed.

The problem, of course, is that if one of the recursive calls to copy() throws an exception, then the node allocated at the start of the method isn't deleted. For completeness, here's one way to fix it by using auto_ptr:

```
TreeNode* copyFixed() {
    auto_ptr<TreeNode> node(new TreeNode(m_value));
    if(m_left)
        node->m_left = m_left->copyFixed();
    if(m_right)
        node->m_right = m_right->copyFixed();
    return node.release();
}
```

The Test Framework

So, how does the framework know how many times to run the test and which exceptions to throw? The heart of it is the Test class, each instance of which represents a single test.

\\ /
~ Joe Asks...

Surely Running Out of Memory Isn't a Problem Anymore?

In these days of virtual memory, running out of memory just isn't an issue. So, why bother testing for bad_alloc being thrown when it'll never happen in practice?

The point *isn't* to check that the code copes when it runs out of memory (although that is a side benefit). The point is to check that the code is *exception safe*. Because most C++ programs allocate memory regularly, checking that we can handle bad_alloc is an excellent way to exercise a wide variety of possible exception-handling paths.

Writing exception safe code in C++ is tricky—much more difficult than it might appear at first. For an excellent discussion of the subtleties involved, see Herb Sutter's *Exceptional C++* (Sut99).

```
class Test {
public:
    Test(const char* name, void (*testFunction)());
    ~Test();

    void run();

    static bool testError();

private:
    const char* m_name;
    void (*m_testFunction)();

    void runInternal();

    // Count of errors that can be triggered
    static int m_errorCount;
    static int m_throwOnError;
};
```

Test maintains two static variables, m_errorCount and m_throwOnError. How these variables control test execution is shown in Figure 10.1, on the facing page. During "normal" test runs, m_throwOnError is set to zero, and each time TEST_ERROR() is called, m_errorCount is incremented.

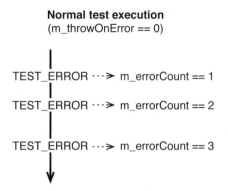

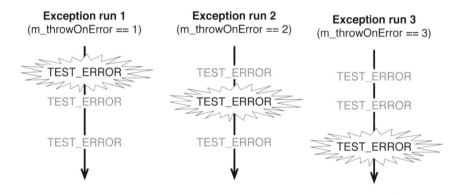

Figure 10.1: TEST_ERROR() IN ACTION

During "exception" runs, m_throwOnError indicates which instance of TEST_ERROR() should throw. Our TEST_ERROR() macro just calls Test::testError(), throwing an exception if it returns true.

```
#define TEST_ERROR(e) \
    if(Test::testError()) \
        throw e;
```

In turn, all that testError() does is keep track of how many possible exceptions we've come across, returning true if the count has reached the value indicated by m_throwOnError.

```
bool Test::testError() {
    ++m_errorCount;
    return m_errorCount == m_throwOnError;
}
```

Here's the run() method, which (surprise) runs a test:

```
void Test::run() {
    cout << "Running test: " << m_name << endl;
❶  m_throwOnError = 0;
    runInternal();

❷  int additionalTestRuns = m_errorCount;
❸  for(int i = 1; i <= additionalTestRuns; ++i) {
        cout << "    exception run: " << i << endl;
        m_throwOnError = i;
        runInternal();
    }
}
```

❶   Test::run() starts by calling runInternal() with m_throwOnError set to zero to ensure that testError() always returns false.

❷   After runInternal() has finished, m_errorCount contains the number of possible exceptions that can be thrown during this particular test, which we take a copy of.

❸   Then, runInternal() is called once for each possible exception with m_throwOnError set to the number of the exception we want to throw this time.

And finally, the runInternal() method simply calls the test after wrapping it up in checks to detect memory leaks and unexpected exceptions:

```
void Test::runInternal() {
    m_errorCount = 0;
    takeMemorySnapshot();

    try {
        (*m_testFunction)();
    } catch(exception& e) {
        // An unhandled exception is only a problem if this is a normal
        // run - we expect unhandled exceptions during error simulation
        if(m_throwOnError == 0)
            cerr << "Unhandled exception in test: " << m_name << "\n" <<
                e.what() << endl;
    }

    reportMemoryLeaks();
}
```

So, there you have it—completely automatic detection of both memory leaks and exception-unsafe code that comes almost entirely for free. What's not to like?

10.4 Put It in Action

- Use assertions to do the following:
    - Both document and automatically validate your assumptions
    - Ensure that your software, although robust in production, is fragile during debugging
- Create a debug build that
    - Is compiled with debug-friendly compiler options
    - Allows key subsystems to be replaced by debugging equivalents
    - Builds in control that will prove useful during diagnosis
- Detect systemic problems, such as resource leaks and exception handling issues, preemptively.

Chapter 11

Anti-patterns

We're all familiar with *patterns*—solutions to common problems that arise again and again.

Anti-patterns are the dark side of patterns—common mistakes we fall into repeatedly. Sometimes they seem to be good solutions that experience has demonstrated don't work in practice. On other occasions, we know that they're not a good idea, but we fall into them anyway.

Forewarned is forearmed. Knowing about an anti-pattern is the first step toward avoiding it.

11.1 Priority Inflation

Early in my career, the team of which I was a member had a problem. As was (and still is) common practice, we were using a bug-tracking system in which each bug was allocated a numeric priority. Our priorities ranged from 1, which was appropriate for trivial bugs of limited severity and impact, to 4, for "drop everything" bugs that took precedence over everything else. So far, so good.

Unfortunately, we had so many bugs that the only ones that were guaranteed to get any attention were those with the highest priority. Of course, people soon worked out that if you didn't give a bug the highest priority, there was very little point in reporting it at all. So, very rapidly we ended up with a database in which almost every bug was priority 4.

This was a problem because all bugs became effectively equal—how were we supposed to know which were really the most important to work on?

Our solution was to create a new priority 5 for "really critical" bugs, which worked for a while. You can probably see the flaw in the plan, though—after a while, we were back where we started, except this time all the bugs were of priority 5.

By the time I left, we were up to priority 7.

Remedies

You can apply a few tactical remedies if you find yourself faced with priority inflation:

- Scrub your bugs regularly. Keep on top of the bug database— review it regularly, and make sure that bug priorities really do reflect their true priority (representative of the value of their fix to the organization).

- Control bug priorities. Allow users to specify *severity* but not priority. Have a well-defined process by which priorities are allocated (a triage team, for example).

- Switch away from numeric priorities, and keep your bugs as a simple list in priority order. This is similar to the *product backlog* recommended by Scrum (see *Agile Project Management with Scrum* [Sch04]).

None of these solutions addresses the root cause—poor quality leading to an excess of bugs. If their number is constantly increasing, no solution that concentrates on merely *managing* your bugs is going to help.

It's not going to be easy, but the only true remedy is to get on top of your quality problem.

11.2 Prima Donna

I once worked with a superstar. He was the "go-to guy"—the team member who could be relied upon to come up with the goods when the chips were down. Very bright and hugely productive—much more so than anyone else on the team—he had an encyclopedic knowledge of the entire product line and could turn his hand to anything.

Management, you won't be surprised to know, loved him. If only we could clone him, all our problems would be solved.

Occasionally there were a few problems with the code he wrote, but these were trivial issues that could easily be handled by lesser team members while he moved on to the next challenge.

If only.

Although on the face of things he was incredibly productive, a cursory examination of his code was all it took for myriad problems to become obvious. It had been thrown together quickly, and it showed in poorly thought-out design, inadequate testing, and unnecessary duplication. The consequences were bugs, both in the new functionality he'd just implemented and in regressions in other areas.

It's a small wonder he was so productive—he was doing only half the job. And small wonder that everyone else was so unproductive—they were spending all their time cleaning up his mess. Of course, none of the dirt stuck to him because by the time the problems surfaced, he was long gone, working on the next high-profile problem that needed superstar attention.

Allowed to persist, this anti-pattern is particularly corrosive. It sends exactly the wrong message. Team members learn that being conscientious is counterproductive. Quick-and-dirty

> Prima donnas destroy teams.

solutions get the plaudits—forget quality, feel the width. Some other poor schmuck can tidy up the loose ends.

Those schmucks, of course, aren't likely to enjoy their role. Their morale is going to suffer, which is either going to lead to poor quality work (why bother—clearly nobody cares) or intensive résumé polishing.

Remedies

Nobody gets to be a prima donna without talent. Potentially they can and should become an exceptionally valuable member of the team. The trick is working out how to harness their talent.

Prima donnas behave as such because they can. Ensure that your development process contains adequate checks and balances, and they won't be able to get away with it anymore:

- Ensure that "done means done." Don't allow *anyone* to move onto the next task until they've dotted every *i* and crossed every *t*. That means all the functionality working, tested, reviewed, documented, and anything else your process calls for.

> \\|/ **Joe Asks...**
>
> **What If I'm Not in Charge?**
>
> An early reviewer of this chapter asked, "These are great ideas, but what if it isn't you (the reader) who decides and management just won't do this?"
>
> Well, some of these processes can be introduced through a "grassroots" movement, and peer pressure can be surprisingly effective. Unfortunately, however, if that doesn't work and nobody in power will take action, then sometimes polishing your résumé really is the rational response.

- Break large tasks up into small, concrete chunks. Treat each individual chunk as either "done" or "not done"—no shades of gray. Five items that are 80 percent complete equals *nothing* done. Four done, one not started, equals 80 percent done. This gives you a true picture of how much progress you've really made.

- Adopt a "polluter pays" policy—whoever caused a bug fixes it. If problems with your prima donna's work come to light at a later date, *they* stop whatever it is they've moved on to, no matter how important it is, and address them. If what they were doing is too important to remain on hold while they're cleaning up their own mess, someone else gets to work on the new project, not the cleanup task.

11.3 Maintenance Team

Some organizations choose to have separate development and maintenance teams. The development team creates the software and then, once it's ready for deployment, hands it over to the maintenance team, which is responsible for bug fixing and any enhancements that become necessary during operation.

If you start from the assumption that the skills required to develop software are different from those required to maintain it, this can seem a sensible way to arrange things. Unfortunately, this structure has a number of problems that lead to a range of pathologies:

- First and foremost, the skills required to develop software are *not* significantly different from those required to maintain it. Software engineering is software engineering, whether you're working on a "greenfield" project or enhancing an existing product.

- The only way to be certain that your design works in practice is to see it working in practice. Some problems will come to light only when real customers are using the software. It's much more efficient for those problems to be fixed by the original designer, who understands the code better than anyone else.

- Related to the previous, how is the designer going to learn how their work fares when it really matters if by that point they've moved on to something else? Learning these lessons is critical if they're not going to make the same mistakes over and over again.

- Although your project plan might call for clearly separated development and maintenance phases, the reality is likely to be very different. Most software has more work performed upon it when it's in maintenance than it ever does during its initial development. There are good reasons for this, not least of which is the fact that users often realize only what they should have asked for in the first place when you deliver something to them.

- You might intend that part of what's delivered with the software is comprehensive documentation providing the maintenance team with all the information they need. In practice, this is almost impossible to achieve, not just because documentation is often the first thing to suffer when schedules become tight. An awful lot of knowledge about the software is unavoidably *tacit information* that is particularly difficult to capture in documentation, no matter how conscientious you are.[1]

- Maintenance teams almost always become second-class citizens. Because of this perceived second-class status, stronger developers tend to find their way into the development team and weaker ones into the maintenance team. This leads to a "them and us" situation. The development team can't understand why those idiots in the maintenance team can't get things running smoothly—the hard work has already been done, after all. And the maintenance

---

1. For a discussion of how communication works within and between teams, see *Agile Software Development: The Cooperative Game* [Coc06].

team can't understand why the development team have (yet again) been allowed to get away with supplying another buggy pile of poorly documented crap.

- If the team that created the software in the first place knows that it's going to be maintaining it, then the team members will be motivated to ensure that it's as easy to debug and enhance as possible. As we've already seen, there are numerous things we can build in at the outset that help considerably. If someone else is responsible, however, the temptation to push this to the bottom of the to-do list can be irresistible.

This anti-pattern also applies to individual developers. Having a new team member work on fixing a few bugs can be a good, gentle introduction to the project. But relegating them to nothing but bug fixing does neither them nor the rest of the team any favors in the long term.

Remedies

Keep one team from initial concept through to deployment.

Make a single team responsible for a product from its initial concept through deployment and beyond. This gives you continuity, ensures that team members' priorities are aligned with those of the whole organization, and allows them to learn the lessons of maintaining the software while it's in production.

Note that a "SWAT team" (Section 7.3, *SWAT Team*, on page 112) isn't a maintenance team in the sense we're discussing here. A SWAT team is a short-lived entity, formed to cope with a specific problem, not a long-term part of the organizational structure.

11.4 Firefighting

Firefighting is a mode of behavior in which, faced with a number of critical problems, we rush from one to another doing just enough to put out the worst fire before moving on to the next.

We're all prone to it. When customers, managers, or colleagues are screaming at you and critical deadlines are approaching, it can seem as though you have no choice. Rarely, it can be appropriate behavior— sometimes you really do just have to do whatever it takes to get the immediate problems out of the way.

It's a big problem, however, if you find yourself falling into firefighting mode regularly or for extended periods.

Remedies

Extended or repeated firefighting will destroy both code quality and team morale. If you find yourself falling into it, you need to take a step back, determine the root cause of the problems you're facing, and address them directly.

This is easier said than done. You *have* no time to search for root causes—you're spending all your time rushing from one problem to the next. It can be difficult to see how you can possibly afford to take a step back and look at the big picture.

Unfortunately, no amount of firefighting will ever dig you out of a quality problem. Quite the reverse, in fact.

> Firefighting will never fix a quality problem.

If you've been firefighting for a week and still haven't gotten on top of things, simply working harder will not and cannot work. Whatever the short-term consequences, you need to stop and allow yourself to identify and fix the root cause.

This may mean that you have to take some unpalatable decisions. You may need to suffer some short-term pain in order to build stronger foundations for the long term (see Section 7.3, *Digging Yourself Out of a Quality Hole*, on page 108 for suggestions about how to go about doing so).

11.5 Rewrite

It can be tempting, when faced with a particularly troublesome body of software, to apply the Alexandrian solution—cut through the Gordian knot by discarding the code and rewriting it from scratch.

Sometimes this really is the right solution, but experience shows that we software engineers have a tendency to adopt it too readily.

From a psychological point of view, it's just *nicer* to be working on greenfield code instead of having to fight against the crusty old stuff. And our natural optimism leads us to underestimate how much effort and time it's going to take to replicate the old functionality.

Old and Rusty vs. New and Shiny

Outside the world of software, my passion is motor racing. As a result, I spend many weekends fettling my race car, performing routine maintenance, fixing damage incurred at the last event, or upgrading components in the search for that last crucial tenth of a second.

I've built a new car from the ground up on a couple of occasions. Compared to normal, it's a wonderful experience. Instead of fighting with recalcitrant nuts and bolts that were last undone years ago and have seized solid in the interim and getting covered in dirty oil and grease in the process, you're working with shiny new components that fit together with ease. If only it could be like this all the time.

But race cars are never fast "out of the box." The first few races, you're constantly finding and fixing teething problems—small issues that either slow you down or mean that you don't finish the race at all. Only after you've sorted all of these out can you extract the car's full potential.

The drivers at the sharp end of the field are the ones who've persevered, developing their cars incrementally over time.

Even if the code as it stands isn't well structured, tested, or documented, if it has been in production for any length of time, then it probably mostly works. This means that it encodes a huge amount of knowledge about the problem domain—knowledge that is unlikely to be captured anywhere else.

This knowledge is the subtle kind that's difficult to recapture during requirements analysis. The special cases that always crop up in production—"Yes, it should *normally* do that, but for records of this particular type, it should behave differently"—may not be captured in any documentation or anywhere else other than the source code. Rewrite the software, and unless you're very careful, you're going to be chasing lots of regressions as you relearn those lessons.

Remedies

Be very suspicious of any proposal to rewrite. Perform a very careful cost/benefit analysis. Sometimes the old code really is so terrible that it's not worth persevering with it, but take the time to prove this to yourself.

If you do decide to go down this road, minimize your exposure as much as possible. Try to find a way to rewrite the code incrementally instead of in a "big bang."

Test against the existing code, and verify that you get the same results. Be particularly careful to find the corner cases that the existing code handles correctly and that you need to replicate.

Avoid "big bang" rewrites.

11.6 No Code Ownership

One of the practices of Extreme Programming (see *Extreme Programming Explained: Embrace Change* [wCA04]) is *collective code ownership*, in which every team member is responsible for all the code. In particular, anyone can fix any bug anywhere in the code without necessarily liaising with the original author.

The popularity (notoriety?) of XP has led to a number of teams adopting the practice, not always within an XP framework. This can lead to problems. Collective code ownership can work extremely effectively, but applied incorrectly, it can easily degenerate into a situation in which there is no code ownership. Anyone can change anything they want at any time, leading to poor quality and even thrashing, in which code is refactored back and forth depending upon the whim of whoever happens to be looking at it.

Remedies

Collective code ownership works in XP because it's supported by a number of other XP practices, in particular pair programming, test-first development, and agreed coding standards. Adopt collective code ownership without these or other practices that provide similar support, and you're in danger.

If you aren't able to adopt such supporting practices, perhaps shared code ownership isn't for you? Consider a more traditional model in which one team member (or a small team within the wider team) owns each module.

11.7 Black Magic

You wouldn't think that we software engineers would be at all superstitious. Software is the most transparent entity you could possibly work with—if you ever want to know why it's behaving as it is, everything you could ever need to work it out is in the source code.

Nevertheless, many projects seem to have their own little bits of black magic:

- "Yeah—for some reason builds created on that server always show that bug. Dunno why, just make sure that you always take the build from that other server instead."

- "Oh, you're getting *that* error. You need to make sure that you start things in the right order. It shouldn't make a difference, but for some reason it does."

- "Yup, the first time always fails, but after that it always works perfectly. Don't worry about it."

The trouble is that anything of this nature indicates that there's some aspect of the software that you don't understand. And anything that you don't understand is a potential source of bugs.

Remedies

> Treat anything you don't understand as a bug.

The only remedy in this case is discipline. Treat anything you don't understand as a bug. Even if, after investigating it, you decide that it isn't a bug, you're sure to learn something.

This chapter has covered a number of common anti-patterns. As you can imagine, it's not an exclusive list. Human ingenuity being what it is, we've invented plenty of other ways to make life difficult for ourselves. Combat this by continually examining your process and structures with a critical eye, making sure that they're really moving you closer to your goal.

In the course of your career as a software engineer, you're going to find yourself faced with software that behaves in frustrating, irritating, obscure, and occasionally downright bizarre ways. I hope that the tools, techniques, and approaches I've covered will give you a little help and the inspiration to realize that you *will* win in the end. The "eureka" moment when you do will repay all the hard work that gets you there. Bon voyage!

11.8 Put It in Action

- Keep on top of your bug database to ensure that it accurately reflects your true priorities.

- The polluter pays—don't allow anyone to move onto a new task until they've completely finished their current one. If bugs come to light in their work, they fix them.

- Make a single team responsible for a product from its initial concept through deployment and beyond.

- Firefighting will never fix a quality problem. Take the time to identify and fix the root cause.

- Avoid "big bang" rewrites.

- Ensure that your code ownership strategy is clear.

- Treat anything you don't understand as a bug.

Appendix A

Resources

It may be trite, but there are good reasons why the saying "If all you have is a hammer, everything looks like a nail" exists. One of the hallmarks of a professional is a knowledge of which tools are available and the ability to select the appropriate one to help with the task at hand. This appendix provides pointers to some of the more widely used.

A.1   Source Control and Issue-Tracking Systems

The problem with choosing a source control and issue-tracking system isn't so much finding one that's right for you as picking through the huge range available. So, what might sway your decision? Some things (not an exhaustive list) to consider include the following:

- Open source or commercial?

- Do you need to host it yourself (behind your firewall, for example), or do you want to use one of the many services that provide hosting for you?

- Do you need your source control and issue-tracking systems to be tightly integrated with each other?

- What level of support for distributed development do you need?

I can't possibly give a complete survey of all the different source control and issue-tracking systems here, but I can give you pointers to a few of the major players and why you might consider them.

Open Source Solutions

CVS: http://www.nongnu.org/cvs/

> Until fairly recently, the only real open source choice was CVS. CVS has a number of well-known limitations, however, not least of which are the fact that check-ins aren't atomic and it doesn't version directory structures.

Subversion: http://subversion.tigris.org/

> Over the last few years, CVS has been almost entirely supplanted by Subversion, which addresses most of CVS's obvious weaknesses and has become the default open source choice.

Git: http://git.or.cz/

> Coming up fast on the rails is Git, which is gaining mind share with a number of high-profile projects switching to it, in part because of its excellent support for distributed development.

Mercurial: http://www.selenic.com/mercurial/

> This is a cross-platform, distributed system with very similar goals to Git and particularly good support for branching.

Bazaar: http://bazaar-vcs.org/

> This is designed to *just work* and adapt to your team's workflow instead of imposing its own model.

Bugzilla: http://www.bugzilla.org/

> For a long time, Bugzilla, developed as part of the Mozilla project, was the default open source choice for issue tracking. Recently a number of alternatives have become available, however.

Trac: http://trac.edgewall.org/

> Trac uses a minimalist approach, aiming to keep out of the way of developers as much as possible. It's particularly notable for tight integration with its integrated wiki.

Redmine: http://www.redmine.org/

> A relative newcomer on the scene, Redmine seems to be well supported and making good progress.

Where open source solutions have traditionally been weak is integration between source control and issue tracking and with development environments. The situation has improved considerably recently with IDEs such as Eclipse providing excellent Subversion support, for example.

Hosted Solutions

SourceForge: http://sourceforge.net/

> SourceForge is the best known of a number of similar sites that provide hosting for open source projects, integrating a number of tools such as source control, issue tracking, documentation tools, and so on. Others include Google Code (http://code.google.com/hosting/) and language-specific sites such as RubyForge (http://rubyforge.org/).

GitHub: http://github.com/

> GitHub provides Git hosting and has recently gained a lot of attention when it started hosting the Ruby on Rails project.

Lighthouse: http://lighthouseapp.com/

> This is a hosted issue-tracking system with integration for Subversion and Git.

Unfuddle: http://unfuddle.com/

> This is a secure, hosted project management solution providing Subversion or Git hosting together with integrated issue tracking.

Rally: http://www.rallydev.com/

> Rally provides Agile life-cycle management tools.

VersionOne: http://www.versionone.com/

> This is a project management and planning tool designed specifically for agile software development. This is also available for local installation as well as hosted.

Pivotal Tracker: http://www.pivotaltracker.com/

> Tracker is a free, award-winning, story-based project-planning tool that allows teams to collaborate in real time.

Commercial Solutions

Perforce: http://www.perforce.com/

> Perforce is a source control system that particularly concentrates on cross-platform support and performance. It also includes a

simple issue-tracking system or can integrate with various open source or commercial solutions.

FogBugz: http://www.fogcreek.com/FogBugz/

FogBugz, from Fog Creek Software, is a flexible bug tracking and project planning tool, available for local installation or as a hosted solution. It's traditionally been available for Windows, but is in the process of being ported to Linux and Macintosh.

Visual Studio Team System: http://msdn.microsoft.com/teamsystem/

Microsoft's Visual SourceSafe has long been a favorite punch bag, criticized for a range of failings. To be fair, Microsoft can hardly complain about this given that it never seemed to use it itself despite its famous policy of *eating its own dog food*. Thankfully, Microsoft's offering in this area seems to have improved to no end recently with the introduction of Visual Studio Team System, a fully integrated source control and project management solution.

Rational ClearCase and ClearQuest: http://ibm.com/software/awdtools/clearcase/

The ClearCase source control system and its associated issue-tracking solution ClearQuest used to be considered the default enterprise choice. They are expensive and complex, however, and inappropriate for anything other than large teams with dedicated support organizations.

StarTeam: http://www.borland.com/starteam/

This is a fully integrated source control and project management system.

BitKeeper: http://www.bitkeeper.com/

This is a distributed system with similar goals to Git.

A.2 Build and Continuous Integration Tools

We've examined at length the benefits of automating your build process, and as you would expect, there are many off-the-shelf tools that will help you to do so.

Build Tools

The granddaddy of build tools is the venerable make. Things have moved on, however, and several much better choices are now available.

GNU Make: http://www.gnu.org/software/make/

> Although based upon make, GNU Make supports a number of significant extensions allowing much more sophisticated control over the build process than has traditionally been available.

Autoconf: http://www.gnu.org/software/autoconf/

> Autoconf is particularly appropriate for open source software that needs to support building in a wide range of different environments. It allows the build system to automatically determine what facilities are available on the host system and behave accordingly.

Jam: http://www.perforce.com/jam/jam.html

> Jam is an alternative to make that typically requires much less configuration to build a given project.

Boost.Build: http://www.boost.org/doc/tools/build/

> Built on top of Jam, Boost.Build provides a standard build system particularly appropriate to building C++ software.

SCons: http://www.scons.org/

> This is a make replacement integrating autoconf-like functionality.

Ant: http://ant.apache.org/

> Ant is a make replacement that has become the de facto standard build tool within the Java world.

Maven: http://maven.apache.org/

> Maven is a software project management tool that does much more than simply manage the build process, bringing package management, deployment, and other facilities to the Java world and rapidly gaining mind share from Ant.

Capistrano: http://www.capify.org/

> Not a build tool per se, Capistrano manages the task of *deploying* software on a number of different servers. Although particularly associated with Ruby on Rails, it can be used to deploy products created with any technology.

Continuous Integration Tools

Many of the proprietary systems we've already discussed (such as Microsoft's Visual Studio Team System) come with their own continuous integration solutions. In addition, there are a number of open source systems available:

CruiseControl: http://cruisecontrol.sourceforge.net/

> This is probably the best known open source continuous integration system. As well as the main Java implementation, there are also .NET and Ruby on Rails variants.

Hudson: http://hudson.dev.java.net/

> This is an open source J2EE continuous integration server.

A.3 Useful Libraries

Not all tools are stand-alone—many, covered in this section, come in the form of libraries that we need to link with our own code.

Testing

The last few years have seen an explosion in the number of test frameworks, many of which are based upon the seminal JUnit. There's no way that I can begin to cover them all here, so I will restrict myself to referencing the "big two" in the Java community:

JUnit: http://www.junit.org/

> This is the library that started it all.

TestNG: http://testng.org/

> This is a more recent test framework, which builds upon the ideas in JUnit but takes a few different approaches and is starting to gain a considerable following.

Debugging Memory Allocators

As we discussed in Section 10.2, *Debugging Memory Allocators*, on page 170, in languages like C and C++ that don't provide memory management, a debugging memory allocator is an essential tool to avoid memory leaks, corruption, and other common issues.

libcwd: http://libcwd.sourceforge.net/

> This is an open source debugging support library that provides memory debugging along with other features.

Microsoft Visual C++: http://msdn.microsoft.com/visualc/

> Microsoft's Visual C++ ships with a debugging memory allocator built in. Search for *Memory Leak Detection and Isolation* in the documentation for further information.

Mudflap: http://gcc.gnu.org/wiki/Mudflap_Pointer_Debugging

> Mudflap is a technology built into some versions of the GNU C and C++ compiler that instruments all risky pointer and array dereferencing operations, some standard library string and heap functions, and some other associated constructs with range and validity tests.

Dinkumware: http://www.dinkumware.com/

> Dinkumware sells C and C++ standard libraries that include comprehensive support for memory debugging.

Electric Fence: http://perens.com/works/software/ElectricFence/

> This uses virtual memory hardware to detect memory overwrites and reuse of freed memory.

Logging

Logging frameworks provide the ability for your code to contain configurable logging that can be enabled, disabled, or increased in detail, typically at runtime and by individual feature.

log4j: http://logging.apache.org/log4j/

> Apache log4j is probably the best-known Java logging library, and ports exist to most major languages.

Logback: http://logback.qos.ch/

> Logback was designed by Ceki Gülcü, the founder of log4j, to be its successor.

java.util.logging: http://java.sun.com/j2se/1.4.2/docs/guide/util/logging/

> As of 1.4.2, Java includes a standard logging API java.util.logging, commonly known as JUL.

SLF4J: http://www.slf4j.org/

> The Simple Logging Facade for Java is an attempt to tame the plethora of Java logging APIs by providing a common interface that can write to different implementations at deployment time.

syslog-ng http://www.balabit.com/network-security/syslog-ng/

> syslog-ng is the most popular implementation of *The BSD syslog Protocol*, allowing log data to be integrated from many different systems into a central repository and rich content-based filtering.

A.4 Other Tools

Finally, here's a quick survey of some other candidates for every programmer's toolbox.

Testing Tools

FitNesse: http://fitnesse.org/

> FitNesse is an acceptance testing tool that allows tests to be expressed as tables of input data and expected output data, described in *Fit for Developing Software: Framework for Integrated Tests* [MC05].

Watir: http://wtr.rubyforge.org/

> Watir is an open source library for automating web browsers allowing automated testing of web applications. It started out on Internet Explorer on Windows but is in the process of being ported to other browsers.

Selenium: http://selenium.openqa.org/

> Selenium is a cross-platform suite of tools to automate web application testing.

Sahi: http://sahi.co.in/

> Sahi is an automation and testing tool for web applications that runs as a proxy server.

The Grinder: http://grinder.sourceforge.net/

> This is an open source load testing tool in which scripts are written Jython.

JMeter: http://jakarta.apache.org/jmeter/

> This is an open source load testing tool in which scripts are written in Java.

QuickTest Professional and LoadRunner: http://www.hp.com/

> QuickTest Professional is an automated functional GUI testing tool, and LoadRunner is a performance and load testing product.

Peach Fuzzing Platform: http://peachfuzzer.com/

> Peach is a fuzzer that is capable of performing both generation- and mutation-based fuzzing.

RFuzz: http://rfuzz.rubyforge.org/

> RFuzz is a Ruby library that allows web applications to be easily fuzz tested.

Runtime Analysis Tools

Valgrind: http://valgrind.org/

> Valgrind is an instrumentation framework for Linux and includes, among other things, memory analysis and profiling tools.

BoundsChecker: http://www.compuware.com/products/devpartner/visualc.htm

> BoundsChecker is part of Compuware's DevPartner for Visual C++ BoundsChecker Suite. It analyzes running programs to detect memory and other issues.

Purify: http://www.ibm.com/software/awdtools/purify/

> IBM's Rational Purify detects memory leaks and corruption within running programs.

DTrace: http://opensolaris.org/os/community/dtrace/

> DTrace is a highly regarded dynamic tracing framework created by Sun Microsystems for troubleshooting kernel and application problems. It is also incorporated in Mac OS X "Leopard," including a GUI called Instruments.

Network Analyzers

If your software relies upon network communication (and it's becoming difficult to find software which *doesn't*), it can be very useful to see what's really being transferred over the network.

A network analyzer (sometimes called a *packet sniffer*) sits on the network capturing and analyzing all the packets crossing it. You can then filter these packets to extract only those that you're interested in and examine their contents. Broadly speaking, a packet sniffer is a low-level tool. It can capture *all* the traffic on the network but doesn't necessarily have a deep understanding of the protocol being used. So if, for example, the communication is encrypted, a packet sniffer is unlikely to be able to display the information being exchanged.

TCPDUMP: http://www.tcpdump.org/

> TCPDUMP is a widely distributed open source packet sniffer.

Wireshark: http://www.wireshark.org/

> Wireshark (previously known as Ethereal) is an open source tool that provides similar functionality to TCPDUMP, but it has a graphical front end and a wider selection of built-in analysis tools.

Debugging Proxies

A debugging proxy is a higher-level tool than a network analyzer, targeted to a particular protocol. You normally need to configure your software slightly differently so that it communicates via the proxy rather than directly, but having done so very often you can get a deeper analysis of the conversation. Some debugging proxies can even view encrypted data.

Charles: http://www.charlesproxy.com/

> Charles is a cross-platform HTTP proxy that, among other things, supports debugging encrypted communications.

Fiddler: http://www.fiddlertool.com/

> Fiddler is a Windows HTTP proxy that, as its name suggests, allows you to "fiddle" with incoming or outgoing data.

Debuggers

In most cases, your choice of debugger is going to be governed by your choice of language, IDE, or tool chain, so there's little value in me providing a list of choices here. There is one particular debugger that I have to mention, however:

Firebug: http://getfirebug.com/

> Firebug has transformed web development by providing dramatically improved client-side debugging facilities. It allows you to inspect and edit the DOM and CSS, as well as monitor and profile network activity, and it provides full JavaScript debugging support.

Appendix B

Bibliography

[Bec02]   Kent Beck. *Test Driven Development: By Example.* Addison-Wesley, Reading, MA, 2002.

[Bro95]   Frederick P. Brooks, Jr. *The Mythical Man Month: Essays on Software Engineering.* Addison-Wesley, Reading, MA, anniversary edition, 1995.

[Car71]   Lewis Carroll. *Through the Looking-Glass, and What Alice Found There.* Macmillan, 1871.

[Coc06]   Alistair Cockburn. *Agile Software Development: The Cooperative Game.* Addison Wesley Longman, Reading, MA, second edition, 2006.

[FBB+99]   Martin Fowler, Kent Beck, John Brant, William Opdyke, and Don Roberts. *Refactoring: Improving the Design of Existing Code.* Addison Wesley Longman, Reading, MA, 1999.

[Fow]   Martin Fowler. Mocks aren't stubs. http://www.martinfowler.com/articles/mocksArentStubs.html.

[HT00]   Andrew Hunt and David Thomas. *The Pragmatic Programmer: From Journeyman to Master.* Addison-Wesley, Reading, MA, 2000.

[iet99]   Hypertext transfer protocol – http/1.1. http://www.w3.org/Protocols/rfc2616/rfc2616.txt, 1999.

[Knu74]   Donald E. Knuth. Structured programming with go to statements. *ACM Comput. Surv.*, 6(4):261–301, 1974.

[Lad03]   Ramnivas Laddad. *AspectJ in Action: Practical Aspect-Oriented Programming.* Manning Publications Co., 2003.

[MC05]   Rick Mugridge and Ward Cunningham. *Fit for Developing Software: Framework for Integrated Tests.* Prentice Hall PTR, Englewood Cliffs, NJ, 2005.

[OW07]   Andy Oram and Greg Wilson, editors. *Beautiful Code: Leading Programmers Explain How They Think.* Theory in Practice. O'Reilly Media, Inc., Sebastopol, CA, 2007.

[ray]   The jargon file. http://catb.org/jargon/.

[Ray01]   Eric S. Raymond. *The Cathedral and The Bazaar.* O'Reilly & Associates, Inc, Sebastopol, CA, 2001.

[Sch04]   Ken Schwaber. *Agile Project Management with Scrum.* Microsoft Press, Redmond, WA, 2004.

[Sut99]   Herb Sutter. *Exceptional C++: 47 Engineering Puzzles, Programming Problems, and Solutions.* Addison-Wesley, Reading, MA, 1999.

[Swi08]   Travis Swicegood. *Pragmatic Version Control using Git.* The Pragmatic Programmers, LLC, Raleigh, NC, and Dallas, TX, 2008.

[wCA04]   Kent Beck with Cynthia Andres. *Extreme Programming Explained: Embrace Change.* Addison-Wesley, Reading, MA, second edition, 2004.

[Zac94]   G. Pascal Zachary. *Show Stopper!: The Breakneck Race to Create Windows NT and the Next Generation at Microsoft.* Little, Brown, 1994.

Index

Agile Techniques

Practices of an Agile Developer

Agility is all about using feedback to respond to change. Learn how to • apply the principles of agility throughout the software development process • establish and maintain an agile working environment • deliver what users really want • use personal agile techniques for better coding and debugging • use effective collaborative techniques for better teamwork • move to an agile approach

Practices of an Agile Developer:
Working in the Real World
Venkat Subramaniam and Andy Hunt
(189 pages) ISBN: 0-9745140-8-X. $29.95
http://pragprog.com/titles/pad

Agile Retrospectives

Mine the experience of your software development team continually throughout the life of the project. Rather than waiting until the end of the project—as with a traditional retrospective, when it's too late to help—agile retrospectives help you adjust to change *today*.

The tools and recipes in this book will help you uncover and solve hidden (and not-so-hidden) problems with your technology, your methodology, and those difficult "people issues" on your team.

Agile Retrospectives: Making Good Teams Great
Esther Derby and Diana Larsen
(170 pages) ISBN: 0-9776166-4-9. $29.95
http://pragprog.com/titles/dlret

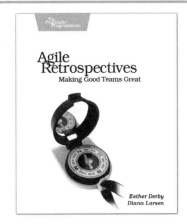

More Techniques

The RSpec Book

RSpec, Ruby's leading Behaviour Driven Development tool, helps you do TDD right by embracing the design and documentation aspects of TDD. It encourages readable, maintainable suites of code examples that not only test your code, they document it as well. *The RSpec Book* will teach you how to use RSpec, Cucumber, and other Ruby tools to develop truly agile software that gets you to market quickly and maintains its value as evolving market trends drive new requirements.

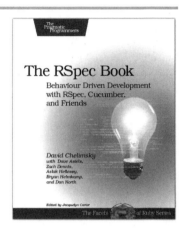

The RSpec Book: Behaviour Driven Development
with RSpec, Cucumber, and Friends
David Chelimsky, Dave Astels, Zach Dennis, Aslak Hellesøy, Bryan Helmkamp, Dan North
(350 pages) ISBN: 978-1-9343563-7-1. $42.95
http://pragprog.com/titles/achbd

Naked Objects

Naked Objects is an open-source Java framework that lets you build working applications by writing just the core domain classes—the framework does the rest. This book shows how you can rapidly develop and test domain applications, and then deploy to either conventional architectures or onto Naked Objects itself. Get ready to write some of the best business software of your career.

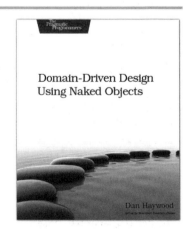

Domain-Driven Design Using Naked Objects
Dan Haywood
(375 pages) ISBN: 978-1934356-44-9. $36.95
http://pragprog.com/titles/dhnako

Develop Your Career

The Passionate Programmer

This book is about creating a remarkable career in software development. Remarkable careers don't come by chance. They require thought, intention, action, and a willingness to change course when you've made mistakes. Most of us have been stumbling around letting our careers take us where they may. It's time to take control.

This revised and updated second edition lays out a strategy for planning and creating a radically successful life in software development *(the first edition was released as My Job Went to India: 52 Ways To Save Your Job).*

The Passionate Programmer: Creating a Remarkable Career in Software Development
Chad Fowler
(200 pages) ISBN: 978-1934356-34-0. $23.95
http://pragprog.com/titles/cfcar2

Pragmatic Thinking and Learning

Software development happens in your head. Not in an editor, IDE, or design tool. In this book by Pragmatic Programmer Andy Hunt, you'll learn how our brains are wired, and how to take advantage of your brain's architecture. You'll master new tricks and tips to learn more, faster, and retain more of what you learn.

• Use the Dreyfus Model of Skill Acquisition to become more expert • Leverage the architecture of the brain to strengthen different thinking modes
• Avoid common "known bugs" in your mind
• Learn more deliberately and more effectively
• Manage knowledge more efficiently

Pragmatic Thinking and Learning: Refactor your Wetware
Andy Hunt
(288 pages) ISBN: 978-1-9343560-5-0. $34.95
http://pragprog.com/titles/ahptl

The Pragmatic Bookshelf

The Pragmatic Bookshelf features books written by developers for developers. The titles continue the well-known Pragmatic Programmer style and continue to garner awards and rave reviews. As development gets more and more difficult, the Pragmatic Programmers will be there with more titles and products to help you stay on top of your game.

Visit Us Online

Debug It!'s Home Page
http://pragprog.com/titles/pbdp
Source code from this book, errata, and other resources. Come give us feedback, too!

Register for Updates
http://pragprog.com/updates
Be notified when updates and new books become available.

Join the Community
http://pragprog.com/community
Read our weblogs, join our online discussions, participate in our mailing list, interact with our wiki, and benefit from the experience of other Pragmatic Programmers.

New and Noteworthy
http://pragprog.com/news
Check out the latest pragmatic developments, new titles and other offerings.

Save on the eBook

Save on the eBook versions of this title. Owning the paper version of this book entitles you to purchase the electronic versions at a terrific discount.

PDFs are great for carrying around on your laptop—they are hyperlinked, have color, and are fully searchable. Most titles are also available for the iPhone and iPod touch, Amazon Kindle, and other popular e-book readers.

Buy now at pragprog.com/coupon.

Contact Us

Online Orders:	www.pragprog.com/catalog
Customer Service:	support@pragprog.com
Non-English Versions:	translations@pragprog.com
Pragmatic Teaching:	academic@pragprog.com
Author Proposals:	proposals@pragprog.com
Contact us:	1-800-699-PROG (+1 919 847 3884)